MW01284894

Ancient Greece

An Enthralling Overview of Greek History, Starting from the Archaic Period through the Classical Age to the Hellenistic Civilization

© Copyright 2021

All Rights Reserved. No part of this book may be reproduced in any form without permission in writing from the author. Reviewers may quote brief passages in reviews.

Disclaimer: No part of this publication may be reproduced or transmitted in any form or by any means, mechanical or electronic, including photocopying or recording, or by any information storage and retrieval system, or transmitted by email without permission in writing from the publisher.

While all attempts have been made to verify the information provided in this publication, neither the author nor the publisher assumes any responsibility for errors, omissions or contrary interpretations of the subject matter herein.

This book is for entertainment purposes only. The views expressed are those of the author alone, and should not be taken as expert instruction or commands. The reader is responsible for his or her own actions.

Adherence to all applicable laws and regulations, including international, federal, state and local laws governing professional licensing, business practices, advertising and all other aspects of doing business in the US, Canada, UK or any other jurisdiction is the sole responsibility of the purchaser or reader.

Neither the author nor the publisher assumes any responsibility or liability whatsoever on the behalf of the purchaser or reader of these materials. Any perceived slight of any individual or organization is purely unintentional.

Free limited time bonus

Stop for a moment. We have a free bonus set up for you. The problem is this: we forget 90% of everything that we read after 7 days. Crazy fact, right? Here's the solution: we've created a printable, 1-page pdf summary for this book that you're reading now. All you have to do to get your free pdf summary is to go to the following website: **https://livetolearn.lpages.co/enthrallinghistory/**

Once you do, it will be intuitive. Enjoy, and thank you!

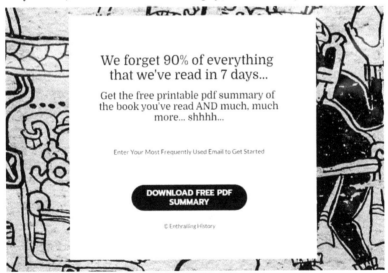

We forget 90% of everything
that we've read in 7 days...

Get the free printable pdf summary of
the book you've read AND much, much
more... shhhh...

Enter Your Most Frequently Used Email to Get Started

**DOWNLOAD FREE PDF
SUMMARY**

© Enthralling History

Contents

Introduction

"Take the joy and bear the sorrow,

looking past your hopes and fears:

learn to recognize the measured dance

that orders all our years."

~Archilochos: *To His Soul*

Majestic palaces lay in ruins in the abandoned, once remarkable, cities. Memories of the extraordinary Minoan and Mycenaean civilizations were fading into oblivion. After lingering in its misty Dark Ages for centuries, with a collapsed social order, obliterated writing system, and lost trade network, Greece was rising from the ashes.

What happened? What sparked this anarchy and dire loss? It's a mystery: when Greece lost its writing system, it lost 400 years of recorded history. Only a few clues supply hints of a great civilization's cataclysmic fall – and not just Greece – several other Bronze Age civilizations in the Mediterranean region collapsed simultaneously, suddenly, and violently.

Did a series of earthquakes or droughts decimate the population? Did barbarian mercenaries rise to overcome their lords, looting and plundering the land? Did the Sea People invade and take over? Archeological evidence suggests a series of calamities – natural disasters, revolts, and invasions – brought the catastrophic end of Greece's Bronze Age, plunging it into centuries of obscurity.

But now, Greece was reemerging – developing a new, exceptional civilization like nothing ever seen before. And this is where this book begins – at the inception of the Archaic period of Greece, lasting from about 776 to 480 BCE.

How was the new Greece organized? The civilization centered around the *oikos* – or family clan – which eventually grew into the *polis* or city-state. The growing population initiated innovative agricultural technology to harvest food from the mountainous, rocky terrain, and Greece was setting up colonies abroad, taking advantage of fertile lands. Greece developed a fresh writing system – this time with an alphabet! Heroic tales, such as Homer's epic poems, were among the first to be written down, dramatically affecting the Greek culture and national identity. The Olympic games and the Oracle of Apollo at Delphi reinforced unity amid conflict. Free speech was now the privilege of all military ranks, and democracy was slowly emerging.

The Archaic period lay the groundwork for Greece's Classical period – which we will unpack in this book's second section. This Golden Age of Greece, from 480 to 323 BCE, permanently imprinted world history with astonishing scientific and cultural achievements. Two millennia later, its democratic political system supplied a model for the United States of America's new government and other countries transitioning to a democracy from a monarchy. Classical Greek philosophers' teachings on democracy and rational thought served as catalysts for advancement in Greece's Hellenistic Age and stimulated change and intellectual progress in the Roman Empire.

Hippocrates taught the revolutionary concept that pathogens caused disease, not the gods.

https://commons.wikimedia.org/wiki/File:Hippocrates_pushkin02.jpg

Why is Hippocrates called the father of modern medicine? He made startling advances in clinical medicine practice during the Classical era. Aeschylus, Aristophanes, Euripides, and Sophocles wrote literary masterpieces that continue to impact theater and literature today. The Greeks built gigantic amphitheaters holding 21,000 spectators for dramatic performances with acoustic engineering that enabled hearing the actors from the top tiers. Sculptors created life-like, sensuous masterpieces of marble, glorifying the human body.

Section three will explore the Hellenistic period, when Greece ruled the known world, lasting from 323 to 31 BCE. Why is this known as ancient Greece's apex? Stupendous advances in math, science, philosophy, and art graced the Hellenistic era. Innovative techniques in architecture and ship-building came into play, along with inventions of water clocks and other scientific instruments. Heron of Alexandria masterminded the first steam engine. Did you know that a scientist first proposed that a spherical earth rotated around the sun during this era?

What united the politically divided Hellenistic world? A common language – Koine Greek – served as the known world's *lingua franca*. Hellenistic culture spread beyond Greece's borders, centering on Alexandria, the capital of Ptolemaic Egypt, and Antioch, Seleucid Syria's capital. Philosophy and spirituality developed in three philosophical schools: the Cynics, the Epicureans, and the Stoics. Through impacting the emerging Roman Empire, Graeco-Roman culture dominated the Mediterranean world.

Understanding the history of past civilizations has immeasurable benefits. Knowledge of the past helps us understand today's world, why things are the way they are, and how the past shaped the cultures and people of today. We know ourselves and other people better. Through learning the catalysts for change in the past, we can experience breakthroughs today. Discernment of how civilizations failed serve as warnings of what not to do in the present.

Exploring the history of ancient Greece is incredibly inspiring. One is motivated and energized by the incredible inventions and advances in mathematics, science, medicine, sculpturing, philosophy, literature, drama, democracy, architecture, and technology. The ancient Greeks were a powerhouse of all things new! What an incredible legacy they left us – things so engrained into our lives today that we scarcely realize how much we owe the ancient Greeks.

Although this book begins with ancient Greece's Archaic period, we cannot ignore the amazing and rich history prior to that era, which flourished in southern Greece's islands and the Peloponnese peninsula. The Greek Bronze Age began around 3200 BCE and lasted until 1050 BCE – when Greeks first started working with copper, later mixing it with tin to produce bronze. Greece's first writing systems appeared in the Bronze Age, and several prominent cultures marked this period: the Cycladic, Minoan, and Mycenaean civilizations.

The ancient Cycladic civilization appeared around 3200 BCE in the Aegean Sea - on the Cyclades islands, where ancient myth said the gigantic, one-eyed Cyclops lived. The Cycladic people - the normal ones with two eyes - fished for tuna, grew olive trees, grapevines, and barley, and raised sheep, goats, and pigs. They carved marble and made copper implements, although they mostly used volcanic obsidian for tools and weapons. They made primitive bronze from copper and arsenic.

The Cycladic people were extraordinary sailors and merchants - significant trade took place among the islands and with mainland Greece - they exported more than they imported. The Cyclades had a dense population in those days; today, only 24 of the 2000 islands found between Greece and Turkey have people living on them. The ancient ruins stand guard over the rest - now barren, deforested, and over-grazed.

The Minoan culture appeared around 3500 BCE but suddenly leaped forward about 2000 BCE, becoming Europe's first complex urban civilization. Its base was the island of Crete - south of Greece and north of Egypt - and included Thera, Rhodes, and other islands. The name *Minoan* comes from the mythical King Minos of Crete, son of Zeus and the Phoenician princess Europa. The Greek historian Thucydides said Minos was the first man to build a navy, conquering the Cyclades, warring against Athens, and controlling ship traffic in the Mediterranean and Aegean Seas. Homer's *Odyssey* says King Minos forced Athens to send seven young boys and seven young girls every nine years to the labyrinth to feed the half-bull, half-man Minotaur.

The Palace of Knossos, built by the Minoans, covers 150,000 square feet. https://commons.wikimedia.org/wiki/File:Knossos_palace.jpg

Crete's rich natural resources and strategic location as a trade hub made it a rich and powerful civilization. Its enormous Palace of Knossos spread over an area larger than two football fields. At the time of their great leap forward, the Minoans started using hieroglyphic writing. Within two hundred years, they masterminded a new script – Linear A – a combination of phonetic signs and ideograms.

Natural disasters brought an abrupt and violent end to the Minoan culture. An earthquake flattened the Palace of Knossos around 1700 BCE. A century later, the horrific Minoan eruption – one of the most significant volcano eruptions in human history, ejecting four times as much as Krakatoa in 1883 – destroyed all life on the island of Thera. Its resulting 400-foot-high tsunami engulfed Crete's coastal regions. In 1200 BCE, an invasion of the Sea People – naval warriors of mysterious origin who wreaked havoc on the Mediterranean – destroyed what remained of the Minoan civilization.

The Mycenaean culture flourished from 1700 to 1100 BCE around the city of Mycenae in the Peloponnese peninsula in southernmost Greece. Mycenae, a city on a hill, was prominent in Greek mythology, which says the Cyclops built its walls with stones no humans could lift. Its mythical founder was Perseus, another son of Zeus, and Homer's *Iliad* said Mycenae's King Agamemnon led the Greek forces against Troy after Paris stole Helen from his brother.

Described by Homer as rich in gold, the Myceneans ruled as an advanced civilization over the Peloponnese and the southern mainland of Greece - including Athens. They used the Linear B writing system, adapted from the Minoan's Linear A system. Exquisitely carved gems, glass ornaments, and vases made from gold, silver, and bronze came from their workshops, The Myceneans were significant seafaring traders - circulating their goods as far west as Spain. Their brilliant engineers built remarkable bridges, complex irrigation and drainage systems, and massive fortification walls.

The Myceneans engaged in piracy, raiding Egypt and the Hittites. Internal strife and invasions by the Dorians and Heraclids, who sacked and burned all their major cities except Athens, caused a decline around 1200 BCE. As the Minoan and Mycenean cultures faded and the Bronze Age ended, Greece entered its Dark Ages, which lasted four centuries until the Geometric culture arose in 900 BCE as a transition to the Archaic era.

The Geometric civilization got its name from its distinctive vases painted with geometric motifs. Trade began to pick up, and Greece was literate again - they borrowed the Semitic alphabet from the Phoenicians. The population significantly increased, and splendid innovations emerged, transforming society back to urban centers.

Now, let's step back in time to 776 BCE and begin following the enthralling Greeks through the breathtaking Archaic, Classical, and Hellenistic periods.

These bird figurines of the Geometric era were buried with a child.
https://commons.wikimedia.org/wiki/File:Bird_figurines._Geometric_period_-_KAMA.jpg

PART ONE: THE ARCHAIC PERIOD (776-480 BCE)

Chapter 1: Rise of the City-States

"Generations of men are like the leaves.

In winter, winds blow them down to earth,

but then, when spring season comes again,

the budding wood grows more. And so, with men:

one generation grows, another dies away."

~Homer, *The Iliad*

Did you know the Greeks believed a great flood separated the Bronze Age from the Archaic era – or the Iron Age, as they called it? One of the earliest-known Greek epic poets of the Archaic period was Hesiod – a shepherd turned brilliant poet after meeting the nine Muses. Hesiod's epic poem *Works and Days* recounts the apocalyptic flood and the Greek's concept of what had happened from the beginning of time in *The Five Ages of Man*.

In the first age – the Golden Age – people had no immorality and lived in harmony, growing incredibly old, never knowing strenuous labor, pain, or grief. The earth supplied food without hard labor. But then Zeus seized control of the world from Cronus, ushering in the Silver Age. In this age, men had to work hard and experienced strife with others, but everyone still lived to be at least 100. Next was the Bronze Age, where the men were savagely violent, corrupt, and ruthless, so Zeus annihilated humanity with a flood.

One family survived. Before rending the heavens, Zeus told the righteous and honest Deucalion to build an ark and prepare provisions. After gathering everything they would need, Deucalion and his wife Pyrrha entered the ark. Then Zeus opened the floodgates of heaven, and the rain poured down, submerging all the land and wiping out the humans. After nine days, the ark came to rest on Mount Parnassus, and the rain stopped. Deucalion and Pyrrha emerged from the ark and offered a sacrifice to Zeus. Their son Hellen had three sons who fathered the tribes that repopulated Greece - the Aeolians, Dorians, and Achaeans.

According to Hesiod's chronology, the Trojan War's age of heroes followed the cataclysmic flood. And finally, came the Iron Age, Hesiod's time – what we call the Archaic era. Hesiod described this age as full of selfish and brutal people who were tired and unhappy. Most of the gods abandoned Earth because so little goodness existed. Hesiod ended his account prophesying that Zeus would one day destroy this world.

But for now, Greece was emerging from the Dark Ages as a thriving civilization - doubling in population in the first few decades. The first Olympic Games in 776 BCE heralded the beginning of the Archaic era, which lasted until King Xerxes I of Persia invaded Greece in 480 BCE.

In addition to Olympic Games, developing an alphabet, and other outstanding advancements, the Archaic era is famous for the *polis* (plural: *poleis*) or city-state in Greece. A city-state is something like a mini-country, consisting of just one city and the surrounding rural farmlands. In the earlier Archaic period, the word *polis* sometimes meant the city's center - where administrative and religious functions happened – not the residential areas or rural suburbs.

The polis center had massive temples and government buildings erected on a high hill – known as the *acropolis (highest point)*. A protective wall surrounded the elegant structures, and the whole thing would look quite formidable yet beautiful. If enemies attacked the city, the citizens could run inside the walls for safety, and the city would fight the invaders from their hilltop fortress.

The magnificent ancient Acropolis still stands in grandeur over modern Athens.
https://commons.wikimedia.org/wiki/File:The_Acropolis_of_Athens_on_Au gust_1,_2020.jpg

Athens supplies a spectacular example of an acropolis that has survived to the present day. The ancient citadel majestically towers above the city on a high, craggy hill. The breathtaking Parthenon – a temple to Athena – was built and relocated and rebuilt several times during the Archaic period, finally destroyed by the Persians. Today, what survives was built in the Classical period, later converted into a Christian church, then turned into a mosque after the Ottoman conquest.

In the later Archaic era, the term *polis* meant a bigger city and several smaller villages and towns under its control – something like a *county* today. Eventually, as the novel concept of democracy became popular in some Greek city-states, landowners became known as citizens – and polis came to mean the body of citizens in a city-state. It referenced the people – not the buildings or land.

The intriguing element of the social/political structure of the poleis of Archaic Greece is that each city-state did its own thing – they didn't all follow the same political and social system. For instance, in Sparta, two kings and a council of elders – men at least 60-years-old – made the decisions for the city, and everything centered around the military. Thebes had an oligarchy, where the aristocrats ran the show, and Corinth started with a one-family oligarchy followed by the rule of good tyrants (yes, that seems an oxymoron). In Athens, they had a developing democracy, and art and education were paramount.

Each city was independent of the other: Athens had no control over Sparta and vice-versa, and the same went for the other poleis. They did not have a central government – no kingdom or empire – encompassing the whole country. Each city-state was like its own small-scale independent, autonomous country. A unified Greek state didn't happen until Philip II of Macedonia took over in the Classical era. They didn't call themselves Greek – but Hellenes – after their mythical forefather Hellen. Even today, the official name of Greece is the Hellenic Republic.

A modern-day example of a city-state is Vatican City. It's in the middle of Rome, but it has its own government and laws, and it doesn't have to follow Rome's regulations nor the laws of Italy!

What bonded all these independent city-states together? A common language and polytheistic religion connected the Greeks (or Hellenes), despite dissimilar political organizations and lack of a central government. Zeus was the king of the gods; the rest of the *Twelve Olympians* – or major gods that made up the pantheon –

were Aphrodite, Apollo, Ares, Artemis, Athena, Demeter, Hera, Hephaestus, Hermes, Poseidon, and either Dionysus or Hestia. A patron deity influenced each city-state – for instance, Athena was the patron goddess of Athens, her namesake. The poleis had a habit of retelling the myths of their patron deity to fit their specific narrative, which partially explains multiple variations of the myths about the gods and goddesses.

Did all these independent city-states get along? No, not really – except during the Olympic Games! Every four years, the *Olympic Truce* – established at the beginning of the Archaic era – guaranteed safety for athletes and their fans to travel in safety to the city hosting the games. No one could fight during the Olympic Games, and no one could attack anyone traveling from and back to their city-states.

As the population grew and spread, ancient Greece ended up with more than 1000 city-states – with the top three being Athens, Corinth, and Sparta. Other important poleis were Aegina, Argos, Elis, Rhodes, Syracuse, and Thebes.

The cities were economically and culturally prosperous, but that led to overpopulation. Greece's rough, rocky, mountainous terrain made agriculture difficult – it was hard to feed so many people. So, the Greeks embarked on expeditions to colonize other lands, creating the beginning of the Greek Diaspora, scattering over a sweeping part of the Mediterranean. They formed colonies as far away as Spain, France, Africa, Italy, and to the east along Turkey's coastline.

Usually, when we think of colonies, we think of a powerful country ruling them from afar. Not so with the Greek colonies – each one was independent and self-governing. Each colony had its own polis. These scattered colonies became immensely wealthy, making them a target of the rising Persian Empire. A volatile clash between the Persians and Greeks loomed on the horizon.

How did the city-states run things, and what were their distinctive characteristics? What characterized their relationship with other city-states? Let's check out several dominant city-states to see how they compared.

Athens is one of the oldest continuously-inhabited cities in the world – about 5000-years-old today! It had been a principal Mycenean center – the only major city in Greece that didn't get sacked and demolished at the beginning of the Dark Ages and flourished instead. In the Mycenean era and the early Dark Ages, kings ruled Athens. In the late Dark Ages, Athens grew wealthy as Greece's leading trade center and began bringing the other villages and towns of the Attica peninsula under its control. Athens – the birthplace of democracy – was the dominant city-state at the beginning of the Archaic era.

And yet, all was not well internally – civil unrest became increasingly disruptive – so the Athenians asked their legislator Draco to write their first written law code in 621 BCE. That was a disaster; the laws were so harsh we now have the word *draconian* to describe merciless laws or law enforcement. For instance, you could get the death penalty for stealing a cabbage!

Solon, who wrote Athens' first constitution, tried to reverse archaic Athens' economic, moral, and political decline.

https://commons.wikimedia.org/wiki/File:Solon_writing_laws_for_Athens.jpg

The Athenians needed to go in a different direction, so in 594 BCE, they appointed the statesman/poet Solon to write a constitution. Solon overturned all of Dracon's laws except the ones about homicide. He divided the Athenians into four classes and gave the lowest class - most of the population - voting rights and other political rights for the first time. Each of the four social groups contributed 100 citizens to the 400-man *boule* (council) - so all classes had equal representation in decisions on everyday life and politics.

Dracon's plan laid the groundwork for *Athenian Democracy* - which gave all male citizens of Athenian ancestry the right to vote and participate in assembly meetings. These rights did not extend to women, slaves, or foreigners, even if their families had lived in Athens for generations. He banned the enslavement of citizens due to debt and broke up the large, landed estates. Solon quickly left town after he finished the constitution so no one could ask him to repeal his laws - and stayed away for ten years!

In the early Archaic age, the warlike Spartans were in a state of civil unrest and lawlessness - still emerging from their Dark Age. Toward the end of the Archaic era, Sparta rose to become the dominant military power in Greece. Sparta became infamous for conquering and enslaving the Messenians of the Peloponnese - which shocked the rest of the Greeks, who weren't in the habit of conquering other city-states. Or, if they did - like Athens, they politely made the conquered people citizens.

The Spartans made the Messenians *helots* -serfs who farmed their lands that Sparta had appropriated and divided the harvest with their overlords. But the Spartans had a problem with this forced labor - the helots vastly outnumbered the Spartans - seven to one. The Spartans lived in constant dread that the helots would revolt and take over. Each year, they would declare war on the helots to kill them and reduce their population without incurring the gods' censor.

The *damos* (or *Spartiates*) were men who had gone through the *agōgē*: Sparta's rigorous training system. Boys left home at age seven to learn warfare, pain tolerance, hunting, singing, and dancing. The schools added in reading and writing later. Sparta divided its land into 9000 equal estates, and each Spartiate had an estate to farm with helot labor – the helots got half the profits, and the Spartiate got the other half. The *Perioikoi* were the free non-citizens – of foreign ancestry – the only ones who could engage in trade or manufacturing – thus, they formed a wealthy merchant class.

Corinth, like Athens, was established 5000 years ago but became a major Greek city in the early Archaic era, with its strategic location where the Peloponnesian peninsula connects to mainland Greece. Renowned for its black-figure pottery, with black animal and human forms on a red background, Corinth accomplished unique innovations in art and architecture. At the beginning of the Archaic period, Corinth did away with its monarchy, and a council of the aristocratic Bacchiadae family ruled Corinth as a group. They had strict *endogamy* – meaning that you had to marry within your *oikos* – or extended family clan.

However, after 90 years of rule, a lame Bacchiadae lady named Labda married out of the Bacchiadae oikos to a man named Eëtion (or Aetion). The Bacchiadeae family received two agitating prophecies that Eëtion's son would overthrow their dynasty, so when Labda had a baby, they sent two family members to kill the infant. But the innocent smile of the sweet, cherubic baby charmed the would-be assassins; they couldn't bring themselves to kill him, rushing out of the room in anguish. Labda guessed what they were up to, so before they regrouped and tried again, she hid baby Cypselus in an ivory and gold chest from the Bacchiadeae baby-killers.

This Temple of Apollo in Corinth, built in 540 BCE during the Archaic period, is one of Greece's earliest Doric temples.

https://commons.wikimedia.org/wiki/File:Temple_of_Apollo,_Corinth,_203013.jpg

When Cypselus grew up, he expelled his mother's relatives from Corinth, then took over as Corinth's tyrant (absolute ruler). We usually think of tyrants as cruel, capricious, lawless rulers – and generally, that's the case. But Cypselus was an exemplary tyrant, popular with the Corinthians, enjoying a long 30-year reign. The rule of good tyrants continued with his descendants, and Corinth flourished under their control.

The city-state of Argos in the Peloponnese rose to dominance in the Archaic era under the enterprising King Pheidon. This innovative monarch invented a standard weights and measures system, developed hoplite tactics and double-grip shields for the military's ongoing battles with Sparta, and minted silver coins for the first time. During the Archaic era, Argos segued from monarchy to tyranny to democracy to oligarchy but managed to prosper through all the changes as a center of industry and culture, even hosting an every-two-year version of the Olympic Games called the Nemean Games.

Pindar was a famous Archaic lyric poet in Argos who wrote in honor of the victors of the Olympic Games. Telesilla of Argos was a famous lyrical poetess who led a unit of women warriors against Sparta. Argos' theater still survives – it could hold 20,000 spectators for dramatic and poetic performances.

The mythical Cadmus, the first Greek hero and slayer of the water dragon, founded Thebes, located in southern mainland Greece (not to be confused with Thebes in Egypt). Herodotus, the historian, said Cadmus introduced the Phoenician alphabet to Greece. Another ancient king of Thebes – Oedipus – featured in Sophocles' tragedy, *Oedipus Rex*. Oedipus killed his father and married his mother, not realizing who they were.

In the Archaic era, Thebes had hostile encounters with Athens and Sparta over the possession of small towns near their borders. An oligarchy – a small group of land-owning aristocrats who made laws, judged disputes, and governed the polis – ruled Thebes.

The city-states defined the Greeks of the Archaic era. They were not one country. Yes, they shared a religion and language – but their citizenship and identity rested in their polis or city-state. They self-identified as Corinthians, Spartans, Athenians – and this strong identity linked to their polis continued even when Greece later united.

Chapter 2: Expansion Across the Mediterranean

"Before the gates of excellence, the high gods have placed sweat;

long is the road thereto and rough and steep at first;

but when the heights are reached (if they are),

then there is ease, though grievously hard in the winning."

~ Hesiod, *Works and Days*

Are you more of an adventurer or a homebody? Can you imagine packing your bags, leaving your hometown, your family, your friends – never to return – getting on a ship, and sailing over the horizon to a city yet to be built? If you survived the horrendous storms at sea, eluded the vicious pirates, and arrived safely at your destination – then it would be time for sweat and toil.

You and your companions, through backbreaking labor, would build that new city and clear the land for farming. You would meet people with strange customs and different languages; some would want to kill you. You would meet all sorts of dangers and adventurers, but if you made it through, you would have unimagined opportunities – a chance for greatness you'd never have had at home. Would you choose the "gates of excellence" – "though grievously hard in the winning?"

Seafaring adventure was nothing new to the Greeks. Most cities in Greece were close to the coast, and from ancient times, the Greeks had roamed the seas – fishing, trading, warring, and exploring. The sea was in their blood. Their mythology featured sea expeditions like Odysseus' wanderings and Jason's search for the golden fleece.

In the Archaic age, Greece was not the small country it is today. In fact, it wasn't a country at all – just a grouping of city-states with the same language and religion. But the city-states extended beyond the boundaries of today's Greece. From the beginning of the Archaic period, the city-states began stretching west to Italy and even farther west to Spain and France, south to northern Africa, and east – around the Black Sea. These were the remarkable colonies of the city-states back home. For 200 years – from 750 to 550 BCE – the Greeks engaged in an organized expansion around the Mediterranean Sea and the Black Sea. Why did the Greeks set sail to build new colonies and expand their reach? Part of the reason was curiosity. What was on the other side of the sea?

But the primary reason was pragmatic: Greece's population was growing fast, and it couldn't feed all the people. Only one-fifth of the land was suitable for agriculture – the rest was craggy hills and mountains. The summers were dry, and winter rain and snow were unpredictable. Crop failure was an ongoing concern – the wheat crop failed every four years or so. Greece needed to send some of their people away so they could feed the rest. They sought out colony locations with fertile lands, so the colonies would grow grain to send home. Not only did this help to feed the *metropolis* (mother city), but it helped ease tensions with nearby city-states competing for land and resources.

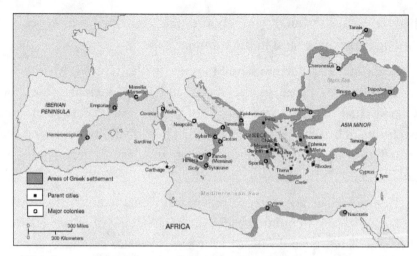

This map shows the Archaic-age Greek colonies around the Mediterranean and Black Seas.

https://commons.wikimedia.org/wiki/File:Greek_Colonization_Archaic_Peri od.png

And let's not forget trade! Metals from Etruscan Italy, grain from the Black Sea colonies, unexploited resources, and raw materials from all over – the colonies were a treasure trove! The colonies supplied Greek-speaking major trading centers around the Mediterranean and the Black Sea, enriching both the colonies and the *metropoleis* (mother city-states) back home in Greece. Colonies flourished in southern Italy and Sicily for five centuries, influencing the rising Roman Republic and enriching and empowering Greece.

How were the colonies established? Who decided to set one up? Unlike migrations in the Dark Ages, where people got into a boat and went in search of better lands, the Archaic-era colonization was an organized enterprise. The metropolis would decide to set up a new colony and would micromanage the details. Sometimes, they would cooperate with other city-states.

How were the leaders of the new colonies chosen? How did they decide who to send? Some of the colonists were volunteers seeking adventure and better opportunities. A few went involuntarily – exiled for disrupting the polis. Citizens from other city-states could join the group. Once a group of people voluntarily or involuntarily assembled as colonists, they nominated a leader from among themselves.

How did they choose where to go? The mother city-state would carefully gather information about potential sites. It had to offer excellent fertile land for agriculture, be teeming with fish, or have abundant raw materials – such as metals. They looked for potential locations that boasted at least two – or better yet, all three – of these prerequisites. Another consideration was whether it was a prime location for a trade center or a stopping-off port for ships sailing to colonies further abroad. Lastly, they had to consider safety and competition. Was the area known for unruly tribes who might invade the new city? Would other colonizing civilizations like Carthage challenge them?

Did they ask anyone for advice while making plans for a new colony? Yes! They went to a very influential woman – the Oracle at Delphi. The Greeks believed the city of Delphi was the center of the world. They had a myth that Python – an enormous snake – guarded Delphi until the baby god Apollo pierced it with his arrows. The serpent fell dead into a fissure, with fumes rising from its decaying body. These fumes would throw anyone above the crack into a sudden, often horrific trance as Apollo's spirit possessed them.

The Greeks built a temple on this spot in the Archaic age and chose a person to bridge the gap between human and divine – the Oracle (a priestess seer) called Pythia. On the seventh day of the month, after fasting and purification, the Oracle would accept questions from any Greeks – it didn't matter from which city-state they came. She would sit above the fissure, breathing in the fumes, and go into a trance. The polis leaders would go to the priestess of Delphi for advice on new colonies, seeking information about the best locations, when to go, and other intrinsic details.

How did they organize the new colonies? They carefully surveyed the new site and thoughtfully laid out the city in a geometric pattern. They would parcel out the surrounding land in equal shares to the colonists for farms. The government of the new colony would resemble their mother city-state - and remember, the various city-states in Greece had different forms of government - oligarchies, democracies, monarchies. The colonies were independent of their founding city-states; they shared close emotional ties, religion, and traditions - but they were self-governing. The metropolis (mother city) had little or no control over an established colony.

What about the people who were already there - the indigenous people in the region of a new colony? Was there friction? Yes, sometimes, but careful forethought went into the location of a settlement, with the attempt to place it in an uninhabited area, or at least not close to fierce warriors or competitive tribes. Occasionally, a mutually beneficial relationship would develop between the colonists and the local people, allowing for peaceful trade. Other times, the colonies took a more aggressive military stance against the surrounding people. And some colonies collapsed in the face of local resistance.

Greece stopped colonizing the western Mediterranean in 540 BCE after the Battle of Alalia. Sixty ships were carrying Greeks to the island of Corsica when a coalition force of Etruscans from Italy and Carthaginians from North Africa attacked them - with 120 warships - twice as many as the Greeks. Although the Greeks drove off the attacking fleet, they lost two-thirds of their ships. The Etruscans captured some of the Greeks, stoning them to death, and the Carthaginians sold the Greeks they captured into slavery. The Greeks abandoned the colonies on Corsica after this catastrophe. The Persians took control of the Black Sea and the eastern Mediterranean, which discouraged Greek colonization in the east.

Which Greek city-states took part in the expansion – in setting up new colonies? The first wave took place in the eighth century BCE, led by the city-states of Chalcis and Eretria on Euboea – a large island just off the coast of southern Greece. They set up numerous new colonies in northern Greece – naming the area Chalcidice. They collaborated with Athens in some settlements, and the city-states of Andros and Corinth also colonized the region.

Different city-states in Greece settled the Greek colonies in Southern Italy and Sicily, each with their own Greek dialects: Sparta and Argos spoke Doric, Euboea, Ionia, Chalcidice, and Chalcis used Ionic, Delphi and northwestern Greece communicated in Northwest Greek, and Achaean was the language of Arcadia and Achaea in the Peloponnese peninsula.
https://en.wikipedia.org/wiki/Ancient_Greek_dialects#/media/File:AncientGreekDialects_(Woodard)_en.svg

The Euboeans were also the first to set up colonies in southern Italy, beginning with Pithecusae on the volcanic island of Ischia – just off central Italy's western coast. Perhaps, they chose this island for their first colony as it had either been a trading partner or a territory of the Myceneans of Greece in the Bronze Age: Archeologists found Mycenean pottery in digs on the island. Although only six miles long and four miles wide, the sea around the island was rich (and still is) with fish, whales, and dolphins. By 700 BCE, this colony had grown to 10,000 people.

Next, they colonized Cumae, on Italy's mainland, just across from Ischia. Cumae had highly fertile farmland, and the Greeks grew grain and produce on Cumae, which they sold to Rome and shipped back to Euboea. They introduced the Euboean alphabet to Cumae, which the Etruscans of Italy modified and started using. Later it became the basis for the Latin alphabet of the Romans, still used today around the world!

Once Cumae was established, it successfully founded its own colonies – Messina on Sicily and Rhegium just across the strait on Italy's mainland, beginning a noteworthy trend of colonies setting up other colonies. Corinth established Syracuse, the dominant Sicilian colony that would grow into the largest city in the Greek world.

In 735 BCE, the Euboeans and some Ionians colonized Naxos in Sicily, across the strait from the toe of Italy's boot, and named after the island of Naxos in the Greek Cyclades. Naxos prospered quickly; after only six years, it set up its own colony of Leontini, followed soon by Tauromenion and Catania – all in Sicily. Athens sent a great expedition to Sicily in 415 BCE, warmly welcomed by the people of Naxos, although other Greek cities in southern Italy gave Athens the cold shoulder. Naxos supplied the Athenians with food and other necessities.

Also, in the first wave of colonization, Achaea and Sparta colonized the Gulf of Taranto at the bottom of Italy's boot. The Greek city-states of Megara, Phocaea, Rhodes, and Crete all established new colonies in southern Italy.

In a spectacular second wave of colonization in the seventh century BCE, Greece set up new cities on the Black Sea, in northern Africa, France, southern Italy, Spain, and Thrace, with Corinth, Megara, Miletus, Phocaea, and Ionia leading the way as the mother city-states. In Egypt, Pharoah Psammitecus I allowed Miletus to set up a trading colony on the Nile – Naukratis – which became hugely prosperous. Corinth colonized the Ionian Sea and Illyria.

"Like frogs around a pond" was how Socrates described the Greek colonies sprinkled around the Black Sea. Although the Greeks once considered the Black Sea inhospitable, the Ionians and Megarons eventually forged ahead to set up 90 settlements on its shores.

What were the resulting local cultures in these colonies? Did the colonists go native or keep their Greek ways? In some new cities, the Greeks assimilated the culture of their new lands – adopting clothing styles, language, artistic innovations, and philosophy. Typically, the colonists would speak Greek, worship the Greek pantheon, eat Greek food, build their cities with Greek architecture, play Greek sports, use Greek science and technology, and enjoy Greek art and theater. Most colonies took part fully in the Greek world. They sent athletes to the Olympic Games and sent soldiers, funds, and ships if their home city-state went to war.

Polybius and Ovid called southern Italy *Magna Graecia* (Great Greece) because of the Hellenistic culture that permeated the area. Usually, they tended to Hellenize or import Greek culture to the places they colonized. This Hellenization would immensely impact Roman culture with democratic concepts, sculpture, pottery, and more.

Pottery amphoras made in Corinth in the Archaic period carried wine, grain,

olives, and olive oil on ships sailing between Greece and its outlying colonies.

https://commons.wikimedia.org/wiki/File:Middle_Corinthian_pottery_amph ora,_Geledakis_Painter,_590-570_BC,_AM_Corinth,_Korm421.jpg

The colonies along the trade routes grew wealthy by supplying a stopping-off point and services for traveling merchants. Some became important trade destinations. What sorts of things did they trade? The Black Sea was a prime source of gold, and Spain supplied other metals – iron, copper, and tin. The Greeks commonly traded food: barley, oats, wheat, fish, grapes, olives, olive oil, and wine – stored in *amphoras* – a clay jar with two handles and a narrow neck. Greece exported exquisite pottery – especially Corinthian and Athenian ceramic vases, vessels made from precious metals, and bronze figurines; in return, they received food items and raw materials for their craftsmen. They also imported lumber from Sicily and the Black Sea region and textiles from northern Africa and the Middle East.

How did the colonies influence culture and art? The routes between Greece and the colonies were communication highways in the Archaic era. As people traveled from one point to another, they transmitted new inventions, customs, artistry, and religious beliefs. The colonies became important artistic and cultural centers – where people would gather from all around, intermingling and sharing ideas.

The colonies set up regional artist schools, reflecting Greek art and naturalistic influences from Egypt and the Middle East. The schools taught skills in carving ivory, cutting gems, crafting jewelry, and metalworking. Greek artists incorporated styles and motifs from the far-flung areas of their colonies, laying the foundations for Classical Greek sculptures, ceramics, and metalwork.

As the colonies grew wealthier and more powerful, they competed in which city could build the largest and most beautiful temples. Lyric poetry (sung to a lyre) became the chief literature of the Archaic period, and the poetry of Archilochos of Paros and Sappho of Lesbos circulated through the Mediterranean.

Athens, Corinth, and Sparta were the leading artistic centers in Greece, and each city-state produced highly-prized, distinctive styles that attracted buyers to the Greek trade-center colonies. Sparta featured extraordinary ivory carvings and bronzes. Corinthian artists gained fame for silhouetted forms in patterns of plant and small animal motifs. Athenian vases displayed mythological scenes.

Did the colonies have competition? Yes – the Greek colonies fiercely competed –sometimes destroying sister colonies. They also faced off with the Phoenicians and Carthaginians – their major trade competitors. In the fifth century BCE, Greek colonization slowed to a halt as the Carthaginians, Phoenicians, and Etruscans became formidable challengers to the sea lanes and new territories.

Nevertheless, by the Archaic era's end, the Greeks had founded 500 colonies, and about 40% of Greeks lived outside of Greece in the Mediterranean and the Black Sea settlements. Many of the Mediterranean's major cities were Greek colonies, some still existing today.

Chapter 3: Sparta and Athens

"The growth of the power of Athens,

and the alarm which this inspired in Sparta,

made war inevitable."

~Thucydides

Which is better – brawn or brains? We remember the Spartans as physically strong and mentally tough, while we consider the Athenians intellectual and cultured. But the citizens of the two competitive city-states were more complicated. The self-restrained Spartans employed canny decisions on the battlefield that might even mean walking away from a battle, while the erudite, aesthetic Athenians developed Greece's incredible war machine. Athens even won more battles than Sparta in the late Archaic age.

Athens and Sparta were Greece's two most powerful city-states but with disparate worldviews, education systems, political systems, ethics, and laws. Athenians were quick, bold, innovative, and progressive, while Spartans were resilient, courageous, disciplined, and conservative. The Spartans valued a strong body and iron-willed mind, while the Athenians treasured thoughtful philosophical discussions.

How did Sparta become a military super-power? They didn't reach that superiority through strength alone – they employed brilliant tactics as well. One tactic included walking away from a battle, and yes – not fighting! They would carefully assess the feasibility of winning – and if the odds weren't in their favor, they would sometimes just go home. They didn't consider this cowardly – they considered it astute. Why waste lives and resources on a venture destined to fail?

An exception to this tactic was King Leonidas I, who held off the Persians in the Thermopylae Pass with only 300 men and a few allies for three days in 480 BCE. Vastly outnumbered by Xerxes' forces, Leonidas and his small force all perished in the bloodbath – but their sacrifice bought time for the rest of the Spartan army to retreat and regroup with other Greek city-states to defeat the invading Persians. Several days earlier, Leonidas had written to Xerxes I, "For me, to die for Greece is better than to be the sole ruler over the people of my race."

In the Archaic period, Greeks began using a phalanx formation, using foot warriors (called hoplites) with shields and spears, covered in armor from their helmets to their ankles. They would stand side by side, with shields touching, forming a rank of solid shields that extended for hundreds of men. Usually, these ranks would be eight men deep to keep the formation from falling into disarray. Most Greek armies used this phalanx formation, but the Spartans had their own spin.

The phalanx battle formation of rows of hoplites (soldiers), shoulder to shoulder, shield by shield, was used throughout Greece.

https://commons.wikimedia.org/wiki/File:Hoplites.jpg

In an *othismos* tactic, they would use four lines instead of eight; the soldiers in the first three rows held their spears overhead to impale the enemy, and the three rows behind the first used their shields to push the men in front of them, to shove their way through the enemy's phalanx. Because they had just four rows instead of eight, this allowed them to fight with fewer men; it also allowed them to spread out more and curve around the enemy phalanx, outflanking them.

The other Greek armies would advance, screaming their war cries and running brazenly toward the enemy. The austere, disciplined Spartans scoffed at what they considered false bravado. Instead, they marched slowly to rhythmic pipes, chanting battle poetry - keeping pristine ranks. This deliberate, menacing approach unnerved the enemy, who would often break ranks and flee before the Spartans reached them.

Another ingenious maneuver was to abruptly stop fighting, swirl around, and fake a retreat. Their foes would break rank to chase after them when the Spartans would suddenly wheel around to annihilate their disorderly pursuers. Herodotus reported the Spartans used this tactic repeatedly against the Persians.

Spartan women enjoyed more power and freedom than other Greek women, able to own and manage property. Girls received a formal education at girls' day-schools, where they learned wrestling, javelin-throwing, singing, and dancing. Women wore thigh-length skirts and played sports – considered scandalous by other Greeks whose women were veiled and draped in full-length gowns. Men married at age 20 but lived in the military barracks until they were 30, making clandestine trips home for lovemaking. Women usually made the decisions in the marriage – their husbands weren't around much.

Spartan focused on its warrior culture, disinterested in the arts and philosophy. All Spartan men served as soldiers from age 20 to 60, and loyalty to their city-state took precedence over family. Teenage boys who excelled in the agōgē training program were chosen for the Crypteia – a specialized force used to dominate the Helots, killing them in annual pogroms.

The Helots – captured Greeks from Messenia and Laconia – were serfs who served as farmers and servants. They received harsh treatment from the Spartans; there were even regular killings to keep their numbers in check. Thucydides described the Spartans inviting the Helots to choose 2000 of their most assertive and accomplished men to receive freedom. The Spartan Crypteia then attacked and massacred the 2000 Helots – the ones the Spartans considered most likely to lead a rebellion.

An oligarchy (a small group) ruled Sparta: two kings and a council of 28 older men who had retired from the military at age 60. The kings were part of the council and had religious duties, but their main task was serving as generals of the army. When the council needed to decide something, they would debate it until they identified two or three alternatives; they then submitted these to the *damos* – the male Spartan citizens – for a vote; thus, Sparta had a limited form of democracy.

Sparta's inland location did not lend itself to sea-faring trade or colonization in distant lands. Sparta expanded by conquering its neighbors and taking their land – starting with the nearby towns of Amyklai and Geronthrai. They then fought a 20-year-war with Messenia, which began in 743 BCE following a local quarrel.

An Olympic Games champion – Polychares of Messenia – leased land from Euaiphnos, the Spartan, to graze his cattle. But then Euaiphnos sold Polychares' cattle, claiming pirates stole them. Polychares found out the real story, so Euaiphnos apologized and promised to pay for the cattle, saying Polychares' son could come to collect the money. But then Euaiphnos murdered the boy! When the grieving Polychares went to the Spartan council for justice, they rebuffed him. Enraged, Polychares began killing any Spartans he could catch unawares, impelling Sparta to demand Polychares' extradition. Messenia said they'd send Polychares as soon as Sparta sent Euaiphnos.

Discussions between the two city-states exploded into war when both sides started bringing up decades-old grievances. The two Spartan kings, needing more land for their people, used the dispute as an excuse to attack Messenia – without warning. In a night attack on the unarmed town of Ampheia, they murdered the people in their beds. This travesty began the war that raged for 20 years, ending with Sparta's ultimate victory in 720 BCE. In the same year, Sparta also defeated Helos in the south, which is when Sparta initiated the practice of keeping their war captives for forced labor – the Helots were named after the town of Helos.

Sparta next turned its attention to Argos, which had allied with most of the Peloponnese cities against Sparta. Argos encouraged the Helots to revolt, leading to the Second Messenian War in 660 BCE, which Sparta won. Sparta realized their survival as a city-state depended on diplomacy, so they formed the Peloponnesian League with four city-states: Arcadia, Corinth, Ellis, and Megara. The league avoided conflict outside the Peloponnese; however, when the

Persians attacked in 480 BC, this league supplied a formidable resistance.

While Sparta was landbound – in the middle of the Peloponnese – Athens had a strong connection to the sea, located just six miles from its port of Piraeus in the Saronic Gulf. On the Attica peninsula between the Adriatic and Mediterranean, with close access to the Black Sea, Athens was in a prime location for sea travel and trade. Greece's mountainous terrain made traveling overland difficult, so Athenians preferred the sea even for domestic travel and trade. Their primary imports were grain and dried fish, timber, cloth, amber, tin, and slaves. They exported grapes, wine, olives, olive oil, figs, cheeses, and exquisite pottery.

While Sparta was an oligarchy/monarchy, its rival Athens was a democracy – at least it eventually *became* a democracy, after starting as a monarchy, then segueing to an aristocracy, then a tyranny, and finally democracy. Five men played an intrinsic part in these transitions.

Historians believe that Athens' kings during the Dark Ages served as the head of the *Eupatridae (well-born)* land-owning aristocracy. The aristocracy formed a council, which met to appoint city officials. In 632 BCE, an Athenian aristocrat and Olympic athlete named Cylon attempted a coup d'état of Athens, supported by his father-in-law Theagenes, the tyrant of Megara – a nearby city. Theagenes had successfully overcome the aristocracy in Megara by killing their livestock – taking away their wealth. Like his father-in-law, Cylon aspired to become the absolute ruler – the tyrant – of Athens.

This portrayal of the Oracle of Delphi is an example of Attic-period red-figure pottery (named after Athens' Attica peninsula), which began in the Archaic era.

https://commons.wikimedia.org/wiki/File:Oracle_of_Delphi,_red-figure_kylix,_440-430_BC,_Kodros_Painter,_Berlin_F_2538,_141668.jpg

Cylon visited the Oracle at Delphi, and she told him to overcome Athens during a feast of Zeus. Cylon misinterpreted this as meaning the Olympic Games, dedicated to Zeus. Cylon faced strong resistance in his coup attempt and fled to Athena's temple on the Acropolis. Cylon and his brother managed to slip away, but his supporters surrendered to stand trial – believing the promises that their lives would be spared. They ended up stoned to death. The magistrates who broke the law of Athena's suppliants and ordered them killed were exiled and suffered a curse that extended through their generations.

Ten years later, Draco wrote his brutal law code. Up to this point, Athens had unwritten laws, which the governing aristocrats exploited unfairly against the people. Yes, Draco's harsh penalties were overly severe; nevertheless, he granted all Athenians equal rights under the law regardless of their lineage, social standing, or wealth. Draco gave the hoplites (military men) the right to vote and hold minor political positions. He paved the way for the beginnings of democracy in Athens.

Several decades later, the aristocrat leadership and the common people asked Solon to write a new constitution. Solon felt that Athens' civil unrest was the fault of the greedy aristocrats destroying the city. He didn't exactly embrace democracy – he tried to find a middle path. "Men keep their agreements when it is an advantage to both parties not to break them; I shall so frame my laws that it will be evident to the Athenians that it will be for their interest to observe them."

Solon's first task was "shaking off the burdens" of debt that enslaved the common people to the aristocracy. He issued a decree canceling all debt, restoring land to farmers that aristocrat creditors had appropriated. He released everyone enslaved because they owed a debt and banned the practice of offering oneself or a family member as security for a loan. He allowed everyone who had fled the city because of their crushing debt to return with debt forgiveness.

Solon's assignment of 100 citizens from each of the four classes to the Assembly supplied equal representation and balanced the power among the economic classes. However, it wasn't a true democracy in the sense of rule by the majority; that would have meant the lowest classes would be running the city-state as they formed the largest population segment. Solon wanted marriages based on love, not financial gain, so he outlawed dowries. He forbade malicious talk about people – even the dead.

Solon reformed the court system to help the lower classes by permitting advocates to seek justice if someone wronged them. His 400-person Assembly served as a court of appeals – which helped check the power of biased judges. His constitution remained in effect for more than a century.

Not everyone was happy with Solon's laws – no wonder he skipped town after he wrote them! The aristocrats lost their power to exploit the lower classes, and the lower classes wanted more power than what he gave them. Some citizens asked him to stay and serve as a tyrant to explain how the laws were to work and change them as needed. But this flew in the face of his ideal that the Athenians needed to make the system work. He was unyielding regarding citizen responsibility.

In 561 BCE, three decades after Solon's constitution, three factions – the landowners, the middle-class, and the lower classes – rocked Athens as they vied for control of the city. A slick, smooth-talking general named Pisistratus gained the support of the lower classes in his quest to be a tyrant. Since the common people were most of the population, he swept into power – ruling for three separate periods.

His first reign lasted five years until opposing forces exiled him. Then his rival, Megakles, invited him back if he would marry Megakles' daughter. But how could they win the Athenians' approval? They got a tall young girl to dress in armor as the goddess, Athena. She rode into town in a chariot – proclaiming she exalted Peisistratos above all men. The Athenians fell for it!

But Peisistratos' second rule was brief – he feared any sons from Megakles' daughter would usurp the position of his sons from his first marriage– so he refused to get her pregnant. An enraged Megakles drove him into exile again – this time for ten years. After growing wealthy from controlling gold and silver mines in Macedonia, hiring mercenaries, and allying with Thebes, Eretria, and Naxos, Peisistratos sailed back to Athens in 546 BCE, overcoming the city-state and ruling as tyrant over Athens until his death – almost 20 years.

As a supreme ruler, Peisistratos promoted Athens as a religious and artistic center, holding festivals, games, music fests, and drama presentations. He taxed the Athenians ten percent of their income, using the money to fund loans and grants for the poor farmers. He improved Athens' infrastructure, built an aqueduct, and rebuilt Athena's temple.

His son, Hippias, succeeded him as tyrant, at first continuing a good reign and reducing taxes to five percent. But after their political enemies assassinated his brother, Hippias became paranoid and cruel. Finally, one of the aristocratic families bribed the Oracle at Delphi to tell the Spartans to overthrow Athens – which they did! Sparta instituted a pro-Spartan oligarchy in Athens, but the Athenians promptly gave it the boot. They installed Cleisthenes instead – Megakles' son!

Cleisthenes, the father of Greek democracy, transitioned Athens from a tyranny to a democracy.
https://commons.wikimedia.org/wiki/File:Cleisthenes.jpg1

Cleisthenes at once initiated groundbreaking democratic reforms. He replaced Solon's four social classes with 139 *demes* (units). The Athens-controlled peninsula of Attica had three regions: the urban neighborhood around Athens, the rural farmland, and the coast that surrounded Attica on three sides. Before Cleisthenes took power, each of these three regions tended to be a law unto themselves. Cleisthenes distributed the 139 demes into 30 groups: ten were coastal, ten were rural, and ten were the city proper.

Cleisthenes assigned these 30 groups to ten tribes – each tribe had one-third from the rural farmland areas, one-third from the city proper, and one-third from the coastal region. The ten tribes supplied 50 citizens each year for the Council, which now had 500 members.

All regions of the Attica peninsula had equal representation, the power of the aristocrats had ended for good, and democracy was in place. Cleisthenes organized Athens and Attica into the political landscape that would carry them through the Classical era.

Chapter 4: From Kings to Tyrants

"The tyrant will always find a pretext for his tyranny."

~*Aesop*

Can tyranny ever benefit a country? Could a tyrant be a moral, exemplary leader? For most of us, the words "tyrant" and "tyranny" evoke thoughts of an evil, power-hungry ruler forcing his will against helpless, oppressed citizens. We're told that tyranny creeps in when good people stay silent, that tyranny is a rule of fear, and that tyranny obliterates freedom.

But is tyranny really the friend of fear and enemy of freedom? What exactly is a *tyrant*? By definition, a tyrant usurps power over a government through force or some other unorthodox manner – not through the usual means, such as family succession, election, or approval of a council. In other words, he's an illegitimate ruler, and any sons or other family members who inherit his throne are likewise tyrants or illegitimate.

A tyrant has absolute power and is unrestrained by law. However, he can use that absolute power for good or for selfish ends. In the Archaic era, people were neutral about tyrants – they didn't consider them intrinsically good or bad – it depended on the tyrant and the city-state's pressing needs.

How did tyrants take over city-states ruled by kings or aristocratic councils? They usually snatched power when the state was in crisis, and the king or the oligarchy wasn't doing much about it. In the Archaic era, city-states faced three predominant challenges. One was the rise of wealthy non-native merchants and artisans; only native Athenians could be citizens, so they lacked political rights. Although they had to pay taxes and serve in the military, they couldn't hold office or have a say in the council – *taxation without representation!*

Another concern was the farmers. Greece had little fertile ground, hardly any rainfall in summer, and erratic rain in the winter. It was difficult for the farmers to get a good harvest. When they had a poor harvest, they would borrow money for food and more grain to plant in the next season. If the next season's harvest were good, they could repay the debt, but if it were deficient, they were sunk!

Drowning in debt, they desperately looked for ways to pay their debtors. Sometimes, they hocked their armor or put themselves or their children up as security. If they couldn't pay, their creditors could take their land, put them in jail, take their children as slaves, or turn the farmers into indentured servants – meaning they had to work a certain number of years to pay their debt.

Greek soldiers had to buy their armor and shield like this fifth-century hoplite (painted on red-figure pottery).

https://commons.wikimedia.org/wiki/File:Hoplite_5th_century.jpg

A third challenge was the changes to the military. As the hoplite phalanx formation became popular, the states began setting up armies – where previously the clans had warrior bands controlled by aristocrat oikos warlords. The hoplite armies cut the aristocrats' military power. Now, just about anyone who could afford a suit of armor could be a soldier – even the non-native artisans and the lower-class farmers. The new military had a democratic effect on the hoplites.

The city-states were getting richer, but the farmers were getting poorer. The foreign artisans and traders were disgruntled because they lacked political rights, despite paying taxes and serving in the military. These unhappy farmers and foreign artisans made up over half the army. In times like these, opportunistic aristocrats – especially popular military generals – would use the backing of their hoplites to grab power, staging coups to take over the city-states.

Although these tyrants had an aristocratic pedigree, they had no hereditary claim to the throne, nor did the council vote them in. They committed "class treason" by setting up a new government that no longer favored the aristocrats but instead favored their supporters – the poor farmers and middle-class merchants and craftsmen. To keep their supporters happy – the tyrants' ticket to maintaining their rule – they would generate reforms benefitting the lower and middle classes.

Tyrants usurped not only monarchies but also oligarchies. Even in monarchies, the king had a council of wealthy aristocrats to advise him. In the early days of the Archaic period, the council had little power. The king would listen to their advice, but he didn't have to follow it – he made his own decisions. But when the city-state went to war, the king depended on the affluent, elite council members to offer men from their oikos to fight and provide them with armor, horses, and provisions.

When the council members realized how much the king depended on their resources, they used this to gain the upper hand over the kings. Sometimes the council would hold the real power with a puppet king. Some councils did away with dynastic succession and elected their kings instead. Some councils had term limits – if the king did not please them, they wouldn't renew his term. By 800 BCE, most Greek city-states no longer had a king – the aristocratic councils ran the show in oligarchies (rule of the few).

Greek oligarchy members were from wealthy families with a distinguished lineage or, in rare cases, from wealthy merchants. Some oligarchies consisted of one powerful family. The upper-class oligarchies ignored the plight of the lower classes – in fact, they often exploited and abused them. This ill-treatment led to class revolts that sometimes ended with the council ejected and a tyrant installed as the supreme ruler.

How did tyrannies function in Archaic Greece? The tyrants didn't necessarily upend the status quo; they tended to keep most of the political system going as it had been. The two things they usually changed were the social and economic issues of the masses. They made everyone happy by building public works – like bridges, roads, and aqueducts – making life easier and supplying jobs to displaced farmers and soldiers.

Tyrants often helped wealthy merchants and artisans gain citizenship, giving them the right to hold office and become part of the aristocracy – broadening its base. They engendered a change in political opinions. Tyrannies were a transitional phase for Greek city-states moving from monarchies and oligarchies into some form of democracy, and they were more common than you might think. Athens, Corinth, Ephesus, Megara, Miletus, Mytilene, Naxos, and Samos are all examples of Greek city-states that experienced tyrants' rule.

Because they lacked political legitimacy, the tyrants could hold power only if they kept their supporters happy. They had to deliver on their promises. If the middle and lower classes became disgruntled, the aristocracy would jump at the opportunity to overcome the tyrant. No tyranny survived for long – they always collapsed by the second or third generation.

Cypselus was the first tyrant of Corinth. His mother, Labda, was from the ruling Bacchiadae family of Corinth. The Bacchiadae had assassinated Corinth's last king 90 years earlier and ruled as an oligarchy, electing a family member to serve as an executive for a one-year term. But the Corinthians were growing weary of the overbearing, arrogant Bacchiadae family, who were exploiting Corinth's commerce to enrich themselves, with a growing economic divide between the rich ruling family and everyone else.

As Polemarch (warlord) of Corinth, Cypselus' valor, fairness, moderate lifestyle, and concern for the people endeared him to the Corinthians. Inspired by a prophecy, he gathered a group of supporters, including his hoplite army, and overthrew the Bacchiadae dynasty. He executed their lawless administrator, exiling the rest of the family and becoming Corinth's tyrant-king. He was so popular that he never needed bodyguards and was considered a mild and statesmanlike ruler.

Some historians have argued that Cypselus was not a real tyrant as he was of royal Bacchiadae blood through his mother. They said he was restoring the earlier monarchy because of an oracle Cypelus received that he would be king – the rulers he overthrew were the illegitimate ones – the true tyrants. It wasn't so much a revolution as a counter-revolution – getting rid of the oppressive oligarchy that had usurped the legal monarchy a century earlier.

Cypselus didn't make innovative changes to the government in place – he supported the status quo. He initiated two fiscal changes: he confiscated the Bacchiadae family lands, redistributing some of them to his supporters, and charged a ten percent tax to landowners. The Bacchiadae family no longer served as the council, as they were in exile (although he later allowed them to return).

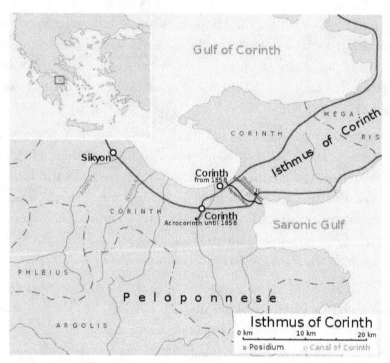

Periander built a ramp over the Isthmus of Corinth to drag ships across – today, a canal connects the Gulf of Corinth with the Saronic Gulf.

https://commons.wikimedia.org/wiki/File:Isthmus_of_Corinth.svg

Corinth's second tyrant – Cypselus' son Periander – was initially known as a wise ruler. Under his reign, trade flourished, especially in Corinthian pottery. He built a four-mile ramp over the Isthmus of Corinth to drag ships from the Gulf of Corinth to the Saronic Gulf – eliminating a long, storm-ridden trip around the Peloponnese peninsula. The tolls from this ramp allowed him to abolish taxes.

But he had a dark side. He kicked his wife, Melissa, down the stairs, killing her. Her violent death caused the estrangement of his son Lycophron, who left Corinth to live in Corcyra, where he became ruler –another tyrant! When Periander was old, he asked his son to return and be the successor to his throne. But Lycophron refused to live in the same city as his father. They were discussing switching cities – with Periander ruling Corcyra and Lycophron ruling Corinth. The people of Corcyra hated this idea so much they killed Lycophron rather than accepting his father as their ruler.

In the example of Athens, the land-hungry city-state was at a tipping point, threatened by strong powers like Sparta and Persia. Under Draco's laws, small farmers who couldn't pay their debts became slaves. They desperately looked for a savior. Solon's debt reform eased their burden, helping to delay the rise of tyranny. But when Solon returned to Athens ten years later after writing the constitution, Athens was literally in anarchy – for two consecutive years, the Senate had not elected an *archon* (chief magistrate). And to his horror, his relative Peisistratus was inciting a tyranny!

Despite Solon's misgivings, Peisistratos was an example of a "good" tyrant – moderate and fair, known for tenderness. He used his own money from his gold and silver mines in Macedonia – along with his new tax revenue – to reinstate farmers to their lands and improve Athens' infrastructure. He enabled the small farmers to transition from subsistence farming to profitable ventures in producing olive oil and wine to export.

Peisistratus' grandson started building this sanctuary of Olympian Zeus in Athens in 515 BCE, but construction halted at the tyranny's overthrow.

https://commons.wikimedia.org/wiki/File:The_sanctuary_of_Olympian_Zeus
_in_Athens._6th_cent._B.C._%E2%80%93_2nd_cent._A.D.jpg

Peisistratus elevated Athens to a maritime powerhouse in the Aegean Sea. The Attica peninsula was a disjointed group of unsupported aristocratic clans that weren't producing much of anything when he snatched power. After his two-decade tyranny, rural Attica emerged as a prosperous community famous for exquisite crafts, wine, and olive oil exported throughout the Mediterranean and the Black Sea. Athens rose to become the dominant trading power under Peisistratos' tyranny, creating a widespread desire for tyrannies in other city-states.

The fierce warrior and enlightened ruler Polycrates ruled as tyrant of Samos – an island in the Aegean Sea – from 540 to 522 BCE. Before his reign, Samos was experiencing violent discord between the ordinary people and the aristocrats. Polycrates, his two brothers, and only 15 men took control of the island. Shortly after – or during the coup d'état – Polycrates killed one of his brothers and exiled the other, making himself sole ruler.

Polycrates built an army of 1000 archers and a navy of 100 galleys – the naval leader of the Greek world. He planned to bring all the islands of Ionia under his command. He allied with King Amasis of Egypt and raided the sea for captives he sent to Egypt to be mercenaries for Amasis. He was little more than a pirate – and he also counterfeited coins!

Despite his buccaneering ways, Polycrates raised the island of Samos to incredible levels of technology and engineering. He built the temple of Hera – one of the three largest Greek temples and constructed a deep-water mole – a causeway that protects a harbor from strong currents and waves. It's still used today by Greek fishing boats! The Samians built the 3400-foot-long Tunnel of Eupalinos – an aqueduct going straight through a mountain – with two teams working from each end, meeting at the middle in an astounding engineering feat that reflected an astute understanding of geometry.

What caused the tyrants to fall? In the case of Athens, after Peisistratus died, the Persian conquest of Thrace and Macedonia by King Darius I slowed economic progress. Peisistratus' sons lost access to the family's gold and silver mines in Macedonia, so they could no longer fund infrastructure programs as their father had done. Their lack of cash made the Athenians feel they had outlived their usefulness – the first stage of failure for tyrants.

Some aristocratic conspirators killed one of Peisistratus' sons, which turned the other brother, Hippias, into what we would consider an archetype tyrant. He lashed back with violent purges until he was driven away and took refuge in the Persian court of King Darius. Now the Athenians had to decide what sort of government they wanted after a 35-year tyranny. Some advocated for the "good old days" of the "ancestral constitution" – which shrewd moderates realized meant a return to an oligarchy of aristocrats and an overturn of Solon's reforms. The moderates prevailed – and followed Cleisthenes on the path to democracy.

How did the term "tyranny" acquire such a negative connotation? This negative attitude began to prevail in the late Archaic era as Cleisthenes reformed Athens' political system. Tyrants and tyrannies came to be thought of as unwanted, despicable rulers. The feeling was that lacking any checks and balances; a tyrant could become corrupt or cruel.

Furthermore, in the fourth and third centuries BCE, the Macedonian king Antigonus II Gonatas gained control of the Peloponnese and installed puppet rulers in the peninsula's cities. The Greeks regarded these "illegitimate" puppet tyrants with disdain and formed the Achaean League of democratic cities to convince the puppet-tyrants to step down. The last mainland tyrant – Nabis of Sparta – was assassinated in 192 BCE.

Tyranny worked well for some city-states in Greece's Archaic era – ensuring stability, bringing prosperity, and helping the poor. It all came down to the issues a city-state was facing and the character of the tyrant. Although tyranny has been much maligned over the millennia, other forms of government – monarchy, oligarchy, and even democracy – can likewise benefit a state or plunge it into chaos.

Plato felt tyranny was a terrible form of government, yet he came to feel the same way about democracy. In democratic Athens, a one-day trial of his elderly tutor and friend Socrates found him guilty of irreverence for the state gods and corrupting the minds of Athens' youth; the court sentenced Socrates to death by hemlock poisoning. Brokenhearted, Plato concluded that even democracy was discriminatory and corrupt, leading to anarchy and bringing the people back to tyranny.

"The ruin of oligarchy is the ruin of democracy; the same disease magnified and intensified by liberty overmasters democracy – the truth being that the excessive increase of anything often causes a reaction in the opposite direction . . . The excess of liberty, whether in states or individuals, seems only to pass into excess of slavery. . .

And so, tyranny naturally arises out of democracy." ~Plato, *The Republic*

Chapter 5: Major Achievements (War, Art, Philosophy)

"You may forget

but let me tell you this:

someone in some future time

will think of us."

~Sappho, *The Art of Loving Women*

Advancement and enlightenment had all but faded into oblivion in the Dark Ages, but the Archaic renaissance recouped what was lost, surging forward to stunning new achievements. Legendary battle strategies, captivating lyrical and epic poetry, enchanting sculptures and ceramics, astounding progress in mathematics, engineering, and science, and the evolution of groundbreaking philosophy marked the period.

Greeks were extraordinary sailors – surrounded by the Aegean, Ionian, and Mediterranean seas, with peninsulas and islands around the mainland. In their many wars, they developed lethal battle tactics for both land and sea.

When the hoplites (heavily armed soldiers) formed a phalanx by standing side by side with shields touching, the point of this battle formation was to power through the enemy's lines, causing them to break ranks. The successful "pushers" would then engage in *melee* (hand to hand combat) with swords. Meanwhile, the phalanx would continue pushing the enemy back. Once they pushed the enemy off the battlefield, the battle was over!

The *trireme* was the dominant warship of the Greek maritime battles of the Archaic age. Agile and quick, it was only about 120 feet long, propelled by 170 rowers and square sails on two masts. It could travel at an average of six to seven knots – about 50 miles per day. Triremes were for day journeys or battles – they lacked holds for provisions or sleeping, so they had to stay close to land. Each rower got two gallons of drinking water a day.

The Olympias is a reconstruction of a Greek trireme – note the bronze ram at the bow.

https://commons.wikimedia.org/wiki/File:Olympias.1.JPG

When they spotted enemy ships, the Greek navy quickly moved into a formation of triremes facing the enemy, side-by-side in an extensive line. Each trireme had a *ram* – a six-to-twelve-foot piece of timber covered with bronze – attached to the ship's bow, which would drive into enemy ships – breaking their hulls – sinking or severely disabling them. The skilled Greek crews knew how to row full-speed and accurately hit the target, then quickly row backward to pull the ram out, so they didn't go down when the other ship sank.

The Greek navy used the *diekplous* maneuver of infiltrating the enemy's battle-line of ships by quickly rowing through gaps between their opponents' ships. Then, the Greek ships would quickly swing around and ram the enemy ships' vulnerable sterns. In a similar maneuver – the *periplous* – the Greek ships would move around the end of the enemy's line of triremes, outflanking them, then ramming their opponents' ships.

Another marine maneuver was *shearing* – the attacking ship would use its battering ram to strike or shear the row of oars on the side of the enemy ship, shattering the paddles and injuring the rowers. This strategy usually caused the ship with sheared oars to come to a full stop in the water, exposing it to ramming. In addition to 170 rowers, Greek triremes carried about 15 to 40 marines who would shoot arrows at the enemy's ships and use hand-to-hand sword combat to prevent them from boarding their ship.

Several famous battles of the Archaic era included the First Sacred War, the early Greco-Punic Wars between Sicily and Carthage, and the Battle of Champions between Argos and Sparta. The First Sacred War was a conflict between Delphi's Amphictyonic League (a religious, tribal association) and the coastal city of Cirrha. The Amphictyonic League protected the Oracle of Delphi – the priestess Pythia who breathed in the fumes from the crevasse and gave advice to people when Apollo's spirit possessed her.

Pilgrims visiting Delphi usually passed through Cirrha's port, but Cirrha was full of miscreants who would rob and assault the pilgrims on the way from Cirrha to Delphi. To protect the pilgrims, the Amphictyonic League laid siege to Cirrha, led by Cleisthenes, the tyrant of Sicyon, who blockaded Cirrha's harbor. Forces from Athens and Thessaly joined Cleisthenes.

Chemical warfare came into play when a horse's hoof went through soft ground and broke an underground pipe. The allied forces realized it was a secret water pipe leading into the city! They put hellebore (a poisonous evergreen plant) in the water, and it gave everyone in Cirrha diarrhea, making them too sick to fight. The League took the city and slaughtered the entire population (or they fled to Mount Kirphe – depending on the version of the story). The League celebrated their victory in 582 BCE by organizing the first Pythian Games – something like the Olympic Games, except that Delphi hosted them. They featured competitions in athletics, art, and dance.

The Greco-Punic wars began in the Archaic era and continued, on and off, right through the Classical and Hellenistic periods. Carthage in northern Africa was fighting the Greek city-states in Sicily – led by the Greek colony of Syracuse – Sicily's most powerful city. While Greece was expanding and building settlements around the Mediterranean, Carthage was vying for the same territory.

Like the Greeks, the Carthaginians were a great maritime people – descendants of the Phoenicians of Lebanon. While one group of Phoenicians built Carthage in the ninth century BCE, other Phoenicians simultaneously founded several colonies in Sicily. When the Greeks started colonizing Sicily in 750 BCE, they had minor conflicts with the Phoenicians and native Sicilians, but mostly everyone flourished through mutual trade for two centuries.

Then Carthage took over the Phoenician cities in western Sicily, while Cleander, the Greek tyrant of Gela in Sicily, took control of the Dorian-Greek cities of eastern Sicily. The Dorian rivals – the Ionian Greeks – controlled northern Sicily, while the native Sicilians hunkered down in the middle of the island, trying to avoid the crossfire. Then the Dorian-Greeks started snatching the Ionian-Greek cities, practicing ethnic cleansing to convert Ionian cities into Dorian ones.

The desperate Ionians called on Carthage for help, allying with them in the First Sicilian War in 480 BCE – the same year the Persians were attacking mainland Greece. A great storm at sea hit the Carthaginian fleet on their way to Sicily, decimating their numbers. Soundly defeated by the Dorian Greeks, Carthage paid them 2000 talents in war reparations and left the Sicilian Greek colonies alone for 70 years.

Sparta and Argo fought the Battle of the Champions in 546 BCE. In hopes of sparing most of their armies, both sides agreed to pit their 300 best champions against each other. The rules were that they would fight to the death – when all 300 men on one side were dead, the other side would be the victor. After fighting all day, only three men were alive at nightfall – one injured Spartan and two Argives.

The two Argives didn't see the wounded Spartan, so they dashed home to Argos, thinking they were victorious. Ashamed to be the only Spartan still alive, the injured soldier committed suicide. The Spartans technically won since they abandoned the battlefield, leaving one Spartan there (still alive when they left the field). With no decisive victory, the Spartans and Argives exploded into a full-out battle with their entire army, which Sparta won.

After 400 years of Dark Ages illiteracy, the Archaic Greeks developed an alphabetical writing system, chronicling their legendary battles, recording their ancient myths, and writing graceful, lyrical poetry. The Greeks developed their new alphabet by borrowing pictograms from the Semitic Phoenicians. *Alpha* (*A*, α) came from the Phoenician pictogram for *alef* (ox) – representing the sound of long and short "a" (ā, ă). *Beta* (B, β) came from the Semitic word *beth* (house) and made the /b/ sound. The new Greek alphabet was phonetic, with letters standing for all the basic sounds

Archaic Greece was famous for its epic poetry: long narratives about the gods and great heroes. Homer's *Iliad* (chronicling the Trojan War) and the *Odyssey* (the story of King Odysseus' journey home after the war) are the foundational epic poems of Greek literature. Hesiod – Homer's contemporary – wrote *Theogony* (the creation of the world and gods) and *Works and Days* (the history of humans).

Aesop lived in the Archaic age as a slave on the island of Samos, writing fables or short stories that usually used animals to teach morality and common sense. Throughout the millennia, Aesop's fables have charmed children and adults. We commonly see and hear phrases and concepts from his fables: "dog in a manger," "slow but steady wins the race," "birds of a feather flock together."

Sappho of Lesbos was a renowned poetess who wrote lyrical poetry – sung to the accompaniment of the lyre or other instruments, the inventor of the Sapphic Meter. She authored poems about love and the family, exploring the emotions of desire and jealousy between women. Same-sex relationships between women were less common than the widespread bisexuality among Greek men – but accepted: Sappho's poetry of lesbian love was immensely popular in her day; for centuries later, her image appeared in pottery paintings, coins, and sculptures.

Solon was a transitional figure in Athenian history: the author of its first constitution and Athens' earliest known poet. His poems interwove political teaching and referred to events of his lifetime: his reforms, Peisistratus' tyranny, and meditations on the human condition.

Tyrtaeus of Sparta was an *elegiac* poet – authoring poems with somber tones about the divine role of kings and the importance of warriors fighting to the death for their city in his martial songs – chants for dances and festival processions.

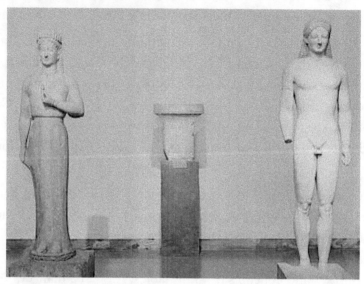

These Kore and Kouros sculptures are from the Attica peninsula. Photo zoomed-in from original.
https://commons.wikimedia.org/wiki/File:A_Kore_and_a_kouros,_two_sphi nxes_and_a_grave_stele._6th_cent._B.C.jpg

Other art forms illustrative of the Archaic period were iconic marble or limestone sculptures featuring muscular nude young men (*Kouros*) and slender maidens (*Kore*) in full-length, yet form-revealing gowns, wearing elaborate braids. The statues were life-sized, realistic, forward-facing forms with ethereal smiles, although stiff compared to the more sensuous Classical-era sculptures. The female sculptures usually had both feet together, while the males had their left leg stepping forward. These sculptures represented ideal youth –beautiful and noble.

In Corinth and later in Athens, the famous black-figure pottery featured both mythological and everyday scenes. The artists who produced these elegant scenes first painted the figures in a glossy slip (a clay-water mixture) on the unfired pottery. After firing, the clay vessel turned red or golden – depending on the clay, and the part painted with the slip turned black. If the artists wanted more details, they would scrape the pottery after firing or paint facial features and other features.

This black-figure pottery, painted and signed by Sophilos, features graceful animals with the gods arriving for the wedding of Peleus and Thetis.

https://commons.wikimedia.org/wiki/File:Sophilos_-_ABV_40_16bis_-_wedding_of_Peleus_and_Thetis_-_animal_friezes_-_London_BM_1971-1101-1_-_08.jpg

In the early 500s BCE, red-figure pottery developed in Athens, replacing the black-figure pottery in popularity. The production method was the opposite of black-figure painting. The artist painted the background in a black slip before firing but left the figures unpainted. After firing, the vase or bowl would be completely black except for the figures, which turned red from the iron oxide in the clay. The artist could paint refined details on the figures with black paint, making them more lifelike.

Some vase painters became renowned for their delicate art, identifiable today because they signed their work. Sophilos of Athens was a pioneer in black-figure pottery, noted for using other colors to paint mythological scenes in unconventional and innovative ways. Two decades later, Kleitias, another Athenian black-figure painter, was unique for his detailed human and animal anatomy and using side-by-side figures.

Nearchos painted this eye-catching oil flask. Photo zoomed-in from original.
https://commons.wikimedia.org/wiki/File:Terracotta_aryballos_(oil_flask)_M ET_DP218738.jpg

Nearchos was Kleitias' Athenian contemporary – both a potter and a painter; he covered his pottery with flowing geometric shapes, using details of men and animals as a border. Lydos was another Athenian contemporary with Kleitias and Nearchos, known for his dignified scenes of "penguin women" wearing black cloaks held together at the chest.

We can't forget the philosophers who shaped Greece spiritually and politically; the Archaic-era *pre-Socratic* philosophers were the intellectual giants who paved the way for Socrates' revolutionary wisdom. Thales of Miletus (in modern-day Turkey) was the earliest known Greek philosopher; he tried to interpret the world's existence and how nature worked through science – not mythology's explanations. Known as the Father of Science, he was a mathematician and astronomer who thought water was the basis of all matter. Thales introduced deductive reasoning to geometry.

Anaximander was a student of Thales in the Milesian school, later becoming the school's master. He was fascinated with the origins of the universe and the first to propose that laws rule all of nature, and we must maintain nature's balance. He also taught the revolutionary concept that the earth floated free without falling – it didn't need the god Atlas to hold it up!

According to Cicero and Pliny the Elder, Anaximander predicted an earthquake would rock Sparta and convinced the people to get out of the city and into the fields. That night, Mount Taygetus split, and the city collapsed. Cicero and Pliny did not mention *how* Anaximander knew the earthquake would happen. What a mind-boggling question! Maybe he observed odd animal behavior? Two days before the Great Sichuan Earthquake of 2008, thousands of frogs (reported by media) swarmed out of the ground in China – and people saw this phenomenon of odd animal behavior elsewhere a day or two before an earthquake. Did Anaximander learn about this potential predictor through his nature studies?

Anaximenes of Miletus was a member of the Milesian school, taught by Anaximander. He believed air was the basis of all matter. Anaximenes thought air's essence changed based on density. Condensed air became wind, which then became clouds, and when the clouds became exceptionally condensed, they turned into water, which rained down on earth.

Pythagoras of Samos set up a school in southern Italy where his students lived as vegetarian ascetics. He was among the first (if not the first) to believe the earth was a sphere – not flat! An astute mathematician, he developed the Pythagorean Theorem: if you square the longest side (hypotenuse) of a right triangle (90-degree triangle), it equals the two other sides squared ($a^2 + b^2 = c^2$).

Heraclitus founded a Greek school of philosophy in Ephesus, where he taught about the *Logos*, which he believed was an unseen force with which humans needed to align themselves. He taught that if humans think they are entirely independent and do not acknowledge the Logos, they are foolish, not seeing things in the true light, and bringing suffering upon themselves. Five centuries later, on the Isle of Patmos offshore of Ephesus, the Apostle John began his Gospel with, "In the beginning was the *Logos . . ."*

Xenophanes of Colophon was a philosophical poet who wrote about religion, the natural world, and how to behave at a banquet. He dismissed the Greek's anthropomorphic (humanlike) deities, pointing out they cheated on their spouses and lived in an eternal cycle of antagonism and drama with other gods. He laughed at the assertions of Homer and Hesiod that gods could be capable of "theft, adultery and mutual deceit." Xenophanes taught that God is incapable of evil. Xenophanes didn't dismiss polytheism outright but wrote about a Supreme God: "One God is greatest among gods and men, not at all like mortals in body or thought."

Xenophanes had a profound effect on Socrates – one could even say his influence caused Socrates' death. At Socrates' trial, the main charge was "failing to acknowledge the gods that the city acknowledges." And they had a point. Like Xenophanes, Socrates lectured that the Greek gods were imperfect and morally compromised. In *Euthyphro,* Plato recorded Socrates' teaching: if the gods committed adultery and deceit, how can we say it's wrong for humans to cheat and lie? How can we have a moral compass with immoral gods? Socrates said his god was wise, rational, and righteous. The Athenians found this to be "impious" and made him drink poison.

The first Olympic Games in 776 BCE spelled the beginning of the Archaic era as Greece was emerging from the Dark Ages. Olympia in the Peloponnese hosted the games as a festival for Zeus, meeting every four years with spectacular feats of athleticism. Around a dozen city-states took part in the first games, mainly from the Peloponnese. Within three centuries, 100 city-states from around the Mediterranean and the Black Sea joined in the competitions.

This scene of runners is from a black-figure amphora vessel.
https://commons.wikimedia.org/wiki/File:Long_Distance_Runners,_Ancient _Greece,_Amphora.png

The games started with foot races, later adding in the long jump, wrestling, javelin and discus throws, chariot races, and military competitions. Better not jump the gun at the starting line – any racers with a false start were executed! Halfway through the games, the priests sacrificed 100 oxen to Zeus, and after the god got his allotment, everyone enjoyed a huge barbecue! The games included an art fair, where artisans, poets, painters, and sculptures would display their talent.

Beginning in 720 BCE, the athletes competed in the nude after one athlete threw off his clothing in annoyance. So, when you see all those naked statues and wonder if Greek men really went around au naturel - well, yes, they did - at least in the Olympic Games!

"But if, my heart, you wish to sing of contests,

look no further for any star warmer than the sun, shining by day through the lonely sky,

and let us not proclaim any contest greater than Olympia."

~Pindar, *First Olympian Ode*

PART TWO: THE CLASSICAL PERIOD (480-323 BCE)

Chapter 6: The Persian Wars (499-449 BCE)

"If a crucial decision is to be made,

they [the Persians] discuss the question when they are drunk,

and the following day, the master of the house where the discussion was held

submits their decision for reconsideration when they are sober.

If they still approve it, it is adopted; if not, it is abandoned.

Conversely, any decision they make when they are sober,

is reconsidered afterward when they are drunk."

~Herodotus, *The Histories*

The year 480 BCE was a critical turning point for Greece – the year Persia subdued most of the city-states on Greece's mainland – with the notable exception of Athens and the Peloponnesian League. Yet this was also the year when Greece transitioned from defensive wars to brazen counterattacks. As we discuss the Greco-Persian Wars, we must step back a few decades to the beginning of conflicts between Persia and Greece. We are fortunate to have invaluable information about the Greco-Persian wars from Herodotus of Halicarnassus' nine-volume work, *The Histories.*

"This is what the Lord says to Cyrus His anointed,

whose right hand I have grasped to subdue nations before him, to disarm kings, to open the doors before him so that the gates will not be shut." ~Isaiah 45:1

https://commons.wikimedia.org/wiki/File:Cyrus_the_Great_II.jpg

Cyrus the Great – Persian founder of the Achaemenid Empire – was the hero of the Jews he freed from the Babylonian captivity – but he was the nemesis of the Greek city-states in Ionia. The clash between his vast and powerful empire and Greece's far-flung city-states began in 547 BCE when he conquered Ionia (now western Turkey) – sending shock waves through the Greek world. The twelve Greek cities of the Ionian League were now part of the Persian-Achaemenid Empire – superpower of the known world for the next three centuries. Ionia had to pay tribute and supply military service for the Achaemenids, but they enjoyed a degree of local autonomy.

The exploitive tyrant, Histiaeus of Miletus, and his son-in-law, Aristagoras, incited a rebellion of all Ionia against King Darius the Great in 499 BCE. Allied with Athens and Eretria, they attacked and burned Sardis, a chief Persian city. Persian troops met them in Ephesus and massacred most of the Greek army. King Darius recaptured Miletus in 494 BCE, and the Ionian revolt crumbled.

Although he successfully subdued Ionia, King Darius of Persia seethed with anger against Athens and Eretria for interfering in his empire. In 492 BCE, he conquered Macedonia and Thrace, then sailed toward Greece. Fortunately for the Greeks, his fleet encountered a brutal storm that annihilated most of his ships, and he had to return to Persia. Before sailing to Greece again, Darius sent envoys to the Greek city-states, ordering them to submit to the Persian Empire. They all agreed – except Athens and Sparta!

Enraged at their defiance, Darius invaded Greece again in 490 BCE. The Persians defeated and razed Eritrea, then sailed to Marathon, 25 miles from Athens. Although overwhelmingly outnumbered by the Persians, the Athenians executed a shockingly bold strategy: they marched out to engage the Persians at Marathon, rather than from behind the walls of Athens. The Athenians, familiar with the territory, fought the Persian army in a swampy, mountainous area, where the Persian cavalry could not maneuver.

The Athenians used the hoplite phalanx maneuver, but with surprising speed, swiftly charging the Persians before they could fire many arrows. After the initial crash against the Persians, they outflanked them. As they circled around to the Persians' rear, the Persians panicked and ran in a frenzied mob toward their ships, some mired in the swamps and others slaughtered by the Greek spears and arrows piercing their unprotected backs. The Greeks plunged into the sea after the Persians, capturing seven of their ships.

The Greeks killed 6400 Persians that day, not including those who sunk in the quagmire, while Athens only lost 203 men. The surviving Persian ships sailed toward Athens, which alarmed the Athenians on the battlefield in Marathon. The people back in Athens wouldn't know that only a few men were on the vessels. What if the people in Athens surrendered, not knowing their army had decimated the Persian forces? One hero - Pheidippides - ran the 25 miles to Athens at full speed - gasping that Athens had conquered the Persians, then fell dead. Athens held firm, and the Persians had no choice but to return home in shame.

Darius was infuriated at the loss but died before he could attack Greece again. His son Xerxes vowed he would not rest until he had conquered Athens and burned it to the ground. Xerxes' uncle reminded him how Athens had soundly defeated his father's tremendous forces. Xerxes had second thoughts, but a spirit visited him that night, urging him to fight Greece. The following night he saw the specter again - prophesying catastrophe if Xerxes did not finish his father's mission. Thinking he might just be dreaming, Xerxes asked his Uncle Artabanus to sleep in his bed the next night. After the vengeful spirit attacked his uncle, trying to pierce his eyes with a fiery rod, the two men decided they had better move ahead with the expedition.

Xerxes' two floating bridges over the Hellespont were built by anchoring and lashing 674 ships together, then constructing a log bridge to rest on the boats.

https://commons.wikimedia.org/wiki/File:Construction_of_Xerxes_Bridge_o f_boats_by_Phoenician_sailors.jpg

Xerxes' forces achieved two epic engineering feats. They bridged the Hellespont (the Dardanelles Strait, which separates Asia from Europe) with two parallel bridges resting on 674 ships lined side-by-side – spanning a mile over deep and turbulent water. In 480 BCE, Xerxes advanced with his colossal force of at least one million men, planning to march across the bridges and then overland to Greece.

But just before his troops arrived at the strait, a fierce storm destroyed the parallel bridges. Xerxes exploded in rage – he had the engineers decapitated, then punished the Hellespont itself – giving the water 300 lashes and branding it with hot irons! The men put the bridge back together, and the mammoth army crossed over and continued marching toward Greece, while Xerxes' fleet of 1200 triremes went by sea.

The second engineering masterpiece took place in Greece. To avoid the treacherous storms off the cliffs of the Athos peninsula, where a storm had destroyed his father's fleet, Xerxes' men had spent three years building a one-mile canal across the peninsula.

Herodotus speculated that Xerxes had the canal built out of pride – pointing out the waste of time and labor since the fleet would still have to sail into the storm-ridden Aegean Sea to get to Athens or Sparta.

As Xerxes and his monstrous forces marched toward Greece, Athens and Sparta allied on this rare occasion! Xerxes marched through Greece with no opposition until he arrived at the Thermopylae Pass, where the Spartans waited. Led by King Leonidas, 7000 men from Sparta and Thebes were blocking the narrow 50-foot-wide pass between the mountains that guarded southern Greece. Simultaneously, an allied navy led by Athens was blocking the Persian navy from the Straits of Artemisium.

For two days, the 7000-man Spartan coalition heroically held off one million Persians. Their brilliant hoplite phalanx maneuver in a constricted space allowed the Spartans to defend the pass successfully. Then a Greek traitor showed the Persians a path that shepherds used to get over the mountains. A squad of Persians climbed the trail, coming down behind the Spartans. When King Leonidas realized they were coming, he discharged all but 300 of his men and some of his allied forces. The other 6000 men needed to stay alive to fight another day. For now, King Leonidas and his forces fought to the last man – sacrificing themselves to hold off the massive Persian army while the rest of the army escaped.

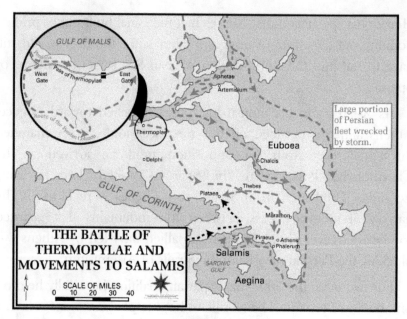

This map depicts the sea journey and the land journey of Xerxes' navy and army.

https://commons.wikimedia.org/wiki/File:Battle_of_Thermopylae_and_mov
ements_to_Salamis,_480_BC.gif

Once through the pass, Xerxes charged toward Athens, but most Athenians had fled to the island of Salamis, preferring their odds in a naval battle. Xerxes sacked Athens and slaughtered any Greeks who had stayed. Meanwhile, the Athenian navy blocking the Straits of Artemisium rejoiced when two vicious storms caught the Persian fleet, sinking half of their ships. So much for spending three years digging a canal!

The Athenian navy, led by Themistocles, won two sea battles against the remnant of the Persian fleet at Artemisium and the Gulf of Pagasae. The Athenian fleet then withdrew to the island of Salamis - offshore of Athens in the Saronic Gulf, meeting up with their land forces and the Spartan fleet. Xerxes' land forces now had control of mainland Greece, but they could not reach the island of Salamis, so the mighty army marched toward Sparta and the Peloponnese peninsula.

The wall built by the Peloponnesian League over the Isthmus of Corinth was a repair or completion of one built earlier. Another barrier was built in 450 CE.

https://commons.wikimedia.org/wiki/File:Isthmus_of_Corinth-es.svg

To get to Sparta from Athens, Xerxes had to cross the Isthmus of Corinth, connecting the Peloponnese to the mainland. But the Spartans and the rest of the Peloponnesian League had built a 3.6-mile wall right across the isthmus, heavily fortified by the Spartans and other Peloponnesian city-states.

The canny Greek naval commander Themistocles sent a message to Xerxes to entice him away from the land battle and lure him into a naval battle in the strait between Salamis and the mainland. The Greek navy tactics were at their best in narrow confines. He deceived Xerxes into believing that Themistocles would betray the Greek forces to the Persians, that the Spartan fleet was abandoning Salamis that night, and that the allied forces were at each other's throats and convulsed by fear of the Persians. He encouraged Xerxes to come to Salamis at once – the Athenians would capitulate, and some would even fight for the Persians.

Xerxes fell for this subterfuge and ordered his ships to sail to Salamis. Interestingly, one of his naval commanders was a woman – Queen Artemisia of Halicarnassus. She urged him to wait – warning him of the elevated risk of fighting in the straits of Salamis. Heedless of her advice, Xerxes ordered his throne placed on Mount Aigaleo to watch the naval battle below – sure that his 400 triremes would be triumphant in the showdown against what he believed were the demoralized Greek naval forces. But all was not what it seemed.

Most of Greece's 300 triremes were hiding out of sight behind Georgios Island. Fifty Corinthian ships were in the Bay of Eleusis, and, on cue, they hoisted their sails in a fake retreat, luring the Persian vessels into the narrow strait. Once the Persians entered the waterway, the rest of the Greek naval forces surrounded them – singing a hymn to Apollo as they plowed into the Persian ships with their battering rams. The Persians were in chaos, with no way to maneuver, trapped by the Greeks. Like wolves, the Greek ships circled the flailing Persian fleet, ramming one ship after another. Floating corpses and wrecked ships covered the water.

Greece's great victory at Salamis – one of the most important in human history – was the watershed moment in the war with Persia. The Greeks were no longer the hunted ones – no longer on the defensive against Persia. Now they were the hunters, and their prey was Persia. At this point, the Greeks switched from defending themselves to launching offenses against Xerxes and the Persians.

As winter approached, Xerxes returned to Persia, leaving his general Mardonius behind in Thessaly with 300,000 soldiers to finish the conquest in the spring. Mardonius knew a land attack on Salamis was pointless, given the wall across the Isthmus of Corinth. But what about Athens? He'd heard the Athenians had returned to their beleaguered city. Mardonius marched on Athens, and the Athenians hurriedly evacuated again to Salamis. Mardonius demolished the walls, houses, and temples that had survived Xerxes' attack. Coming to Athens' defense, the Spartans and their allies marched on Mardonius, who retreated into Boeotia in Greece's mainland.

In the brutal Battle of Plataea, Mardonius attempted to draw the Spartans to low ground. But the Greeks knew better! They stayed in the hills and mountains, where the cavalry could not easily reach them. The Persians cut off their food and water supplies and tried to take the individual hills, but the Greek hoplites outmaneuvered Mardonius' men. The Spartans' phalanx pushed through the Persian lines and killed Mardonius, routing the Persians: 40,000 escaped, but the Greeks massacred the rest of the 260,000 Persian troops.

Meanwhile, the Athenian fleet sailed across the Aegean Sea to Ionia to join the rest of the allied Greek navy. When the Greek navy in Ionia heard the exciting news of their fellow Greeks' great victory at Plataea, they immediately sailed out to crush the Persian navy. The Persians had not repaired all their damaged ships from the debacle in Greece months earlier. Instead of engaging the Greeks at sea, they pulled their vessels up on the beach under the slopes of Mount Mycale, where Xerxes' army of 60,000 soldiers built a barricade around the fleet.

The Greek allies jumped out of their ships to attack the Persian camp. The Persians were confident they could extinguish the several thousand Greek marines, so they came out to fight in the Battle of Mycale. They were unnerved to discover the allied Greek naval forces knew how to fight on both sea and land, trained in the famous hoplite phalanx. Although horrendously outnumbered, the zealous Greeks used their indomitable phalanx to demolish the Persian army, who fled, leaving their ships behind. The Greeks burned the Persian fleet, shattering Xerxes' naval power and leaving the allied Greek navy to rule the seas.

Following Xerxes' defeat in Ionia, Sparta's King Leotychidas suggested that the Ionian Greeks emigrate to the Greek mainland for safety from Persia's attacks. The aggrieved Ionians rejected this proposal – they had colonized Ionia 600 years earlier and weren't going anywhere! Instead, the feisty Greek city-states of Ionia and other coastal cities and islands of the Aegean Sea formed the Delian League in 478 BCE to maintain their autonomy and launch offensives against Persia – placing the Ionian's ancestral city of Athens as their *hegemon* (head).

Cimon, a hero of Marathon and Salamis, served as Athens' navy admiral and the Delian League's commander while building Athens' dynamic maritime empire. With ransom collected from his Persian prisoners, he hosted a simple dinner in his home every day for the poor. When he and his companions met impoverished elderly men, they would slip off their resplendent robes to clothe them and slip money into their hands.

The Persians were amassing a megalithic army and navy in Asia Minor – planning a stupendous offensive against the Greeks. In 466 BCE, Cimon launched a preemptive strike in the double-battle of land and sea on the Eurymedon River in Pamphylia. He destroyed 200 Persian triremes and routed their army. The demoralized Persians left the Aegean Sea in peace for fifteen years.

Hellenistic Egypt revolted against the Persian domination of Artaxerxes I in 460 BCE, and Athens' leader Pericles sailed to their aid with 250 ships. When Athens and Egypt besieged the Persians' *White Castle* (Memphis), Artaxerxes tried to bribe Sparta to attack Athens, so Pericles would leave to defend his city. When Sparta refused to take the bait, he trained and sent a 300,000-man army and 300 triremes to Egypt, capturing or killing 20,000 Athenians and decimating their fleet.

On the way to Egypt, Pericles had taken the island of Cyprus. Once Artaxerxes settled affairs with the Egyptians, he sent his fleet to recapture Cyprus. Athens sent General Cimon and 200 ships in 451 BCE to counterattack the Persians. Although Cimon died during the battle, Greece defeated Persia on both land and sea, ending the Greco-Persian wars.

The Delian League and Persia agreed to the 30-year Callias Peace treaty in 449 BCE, negotiated by and named after the Athenian political leader Callias. The treaty acknowledged the Greek city-states' independence in Ionia and elsewhere in Asia Minor but prohibited the Greeks from interfering with Persian lands in Asia Minor, Egypt, or Cyprus. It banned Persian ships from entering the Aegean Sea, and Persian satraps (governors) could not come within a 3-day walking journey of the Aegean.

Both Persia and Greece respected the Callias Peace, not engaging in overt warfare after its establishment. But Persia continued with intrigues meant to destabilize the already rocky relations between Athens and Sparta. Eventually, the simmering rivalry between Athens and Sparta, stoked by Persia, erupted into the Peloponnesian War.

Chapter 7: The Golden Age of Athens

"We are rather a pattern to others than imitators ourselves."

~Pericles, *The Funeral Oration*

Athens was at its pinnacle of glory in its Golden Age – beginning from its watershed in the Greco-Persian wars when the tide turned toward Greek victory – and extending to the explosion of the Peloponnesian Wars. Its citizens enjoyed peace from war's chaos and embraced cultural and economic prosperity as art, literature, theater, and philosophy reached their peak. This was the "Age of Pericles," who carried the foundations of democracy to new heights.

Cleisthenes championed a democratic political system for Athens. With the Oracle of Delphi's blessing and Sparta's aid, he overthrew Hippias, the tyrant. However, Sparta's King Cleomenes I installed Cleisthenes' rival – Isagoras – as Athens' ruler. Isagoras got Cleisthenes exiled because of a family curse that went back eight decades to Cylon's failed coup d'état when Cleisthenes' ancestors killed the would-be dictator's supporters – suppliants of the goddess Athena.

The Athenians quickly realized Isagoras was a worse curse – he exiled 700 Athenian families – appropriating their property, claiming they were also under a curse. He tried to do away with Athens' citizen council – the *Boule*, but the council and the Athenian citizens firmly resisted. Finally, the exasperated Athenians chased Isagoras to the Acropolis, where he and his backers holed up for two days until the citizens officially banished him.

Athens welcomed the return of those exiled by Isagoras, especially Cleisthenes, who became the next leader. Cleisthenes immediately started the democratic reforms outlined in chapter three, which broke the power of the upper-class families and formed ten new tribes based on location, equally represented by all social classes.

From Athens' Golden Age, this red-figure amphora depicts a Greek hoplite on the left fighting a Persian archer (for which the Persian forces were famous).

https://commons.wikimedia.org/wiki/File:Terracotta_Nolan_amphora_(jar)_MET_DT229457.jpg

The First Athenian Alliance (the Delian League), formed to repel the Persians, was the catalyst for Athens' great sea empire. Amid the Greco-Persian Wars, a stunning discovery of a rich silver lode in Laurium – close to Athens – led to the question, "What do we do with this unexpected wealth?" Predicting that Athens' future was on the sea, Themistocles recommended they build a fleet of ships – and they did! Themistocles led them to the great naval victory of Salamis – the turning point of the Greco-Persian Wars.

Shortly after, the Delian League formed in 477 BCE: each city-state supplied warships, materials, or money to fight the Achaemenid Empire. Athens assumed leadership and swept the Persians out of the Aegean Sea. Cimon, who fought with Themistocles at Salamis, became the League's commander, winning extraordinary victories and more territory for Athens. He drove the irksome Dolopian pirates off the island of Syros, ensuring peaceful trade on the Aegean.

Plutarch mentioned how Cimon loved to tell the story of what happened after successful battles in Sestos and Byzantium. He and the allies had many *barbarian* (non-Greek) prisoners and considerable booty. When discussing how to divide the spoils of war, he told the partners they could choose all the loot or all the prisoners. The allies laughed, "We'll take the gold jewelry and purple robes – those aristocrat prisoners are unused to labor and will be worthless slaves!"

Shortly after, the families and friends of the prisoners paid a great ransom to get their relatives back, making Cimon incredibly wealthy! But he didn't spend it on himself – preferring to live frugally, "like the Spartans." Instead, he supported his naval fleet, put money in Athens' treasury, and fed the poor in his house every day.

Pericles' name meant *surrounded by glory*, an apt prophecy. Called the *first citizen of Athens* by the historian Thucydides (his contemporary), Pericles profoundly restructured Athens' constitution and government, reforming the lives of Athenians with rule by "the many instead of the few." Civil service positions were now open to citizens from all social classes, and paid jury service made it possible for the poor and middle classes to participate in the court system.

This bust of Pericles is a Roman copy of the original Greek sculpture circa 430 BCE.

https://commons.wikimedia.org/wiki/File:Pericles_Pio-Clementino_Inv269_n4.jpg

As a young man, Pericles was a deputy of Ephialtes, an early leader of Athens' democratic movement. Ephialtes stripped the power of the aristocratic Areopagus council and launched Athens on the path toward radical democracy. He instituted pay for civil servants and made it easier to become a citizen of Athens.

Ephialtes' assassination in 461 BCE left Pericles as Athens' leading politician for the next three decades.

Pericles promoted "radical democracy" – meaning the state paid middle-class and lower-class Athenians for taking part in public administration. Before that, only wealthy Athenians engaged in politics because everyone else had to work – they couldn't take time to run the city or sit on jury trials. Pericles believed all citizens should participate in public affairs.

Through supporting architecture, arts, democracy, and philosophy, Pericles ushered Athens into its Golden Age. Athens was the center of the known world's intellectual and artistic endeavors of the day, nurturing breathtaking innovation in literature, stage performances, fine sculpture, architecture, philosophy, medicine, math, and science. Elegant aesthetics – the city's graceful architecture and stirring sculptures that reflected a love of beauty – defined Athens.

The "Father of Medicine," Hippocrates made long-lasting contributions to medical science, including clinical observation, prognosis, and systematically categorizing disease. Hippocrates believed the body could rebalance and heal itself, and the doctor's function was to enhance this natural process. He promoted fasting for some conditions (saying that eating only feeds the sickness) and used a honey-vinegar mix for other illnesses. Part of his clinical diagnosis included careful observation of a person's pulse, temperature, range of motion, complexion, pain level, urine, and bowel movements.

Athenians were intrigued by the ways mathematics affected the real world. They achieved astounding progress in mathematical proofs and theories. Theaetetus of Athens made brilliant advances in geometry – notably in irrational lengths and Platonic solids, paving the way for Euclid's mathematical treatise, *Elements*, several decades later. Socrates and Plato were Euclid's friends, and Plato cast him as the central character in his Socratic dialogue.

Athen's most important religious festival was the Panathenaea observance honoring Athena, which included the Panathenaic Games. Beginning in 566 BCE, Athens hosted the celebration every four years with many sacrifices to various deities – especially to the goddess Athena. Excitement surrounded the athletic competitions, poetic performances, and music contests held in the Panathenaic Stadium. Rebuilt and refurbished, the stadium is still in use today!

Another important Athenian festival was the Dionysia, in honor of the god Dionysius. It opened with a grand procession, with men holding phallic images aloft on long poles. When an idol of Dionysius first came to Athens, the people rejected the new god, so Dionysius struck them with a genital plague. Quickly convinced to worship Dionysius, the men's genitals became healthy again: hence the penis parade.

The bulls for sacrifice were also in the procession; after the priests sacrificed them, everyone enjoyed a grand feast, followed by competitions in dancing and singing. This annual festival featured dramatic performances – originally tragedies, but after 487 BCE, the festival included comedies. The Theatre of Dionysius, big enough for 17,000 people, held the dramas.

The Erechtheion on the Acropolis was a temple to several gods, including Poseidon and Athena.
https://commons.wikimedia.org/wiki/File:Caryatids_of_Erechtheion_(20419 658495).jpg

A high, craggy hill – called the Sacred Rock – stood in Athens' center. From ancient times, a temple-governmental complex called the Acropolis stood on the hilltop, surrounded by centuries-old massive walls – until the Persians sacked Athens in 480 BCE, pulled down the walls, and ravaged the Acropolis. After the war, Cimon ordered the walls rebuilt, and several years later, Pericles engaged in a monumental rebuilding of the Acropolis.

Pericles started with the Parthenon – Athena's elegant temple – the city's new iconic symbol. The Parthenon's central room held a 40-foot ivory and gold idol of the Athena Parthenos (virgin), sculptured by the famous artist Phidias – Pericles' good friend. The goddess embodied Athens' prowess in war, knowledge, reason, and aesthetics. Athena's temple had panels on all four sides with friezes illustrating famous Greek myths: the Trojan War and battles with centaurs, giants, and Amazon warrior women.

In 437 BCE, construction began on the Propylaea – a stupendous marble gate of Doric colonnades. Behind this gate stood a 30-foot bronze sculpture of the Athena *Promachos* (*she fights on the front line*), holding a spear and a shield. Situated on the Sacred Hill, the reflection of this tall statue could be seen three miles away at the coast. Scattered over the Acropolis were temples to other gods.

As Athens' leader, Pericles held great power over the Delian League, compelling tribute payments of ships, money, or materials from the 330-member city-states (some forced to be members). Initially, the League's treasury was kept at the sacred island of Delos – the League's namesake. In the beginning, each city-state paid 460 talents – or the equivalent in grain, ships, timber, or other materials, but in 425 BCE, the tribute went up to 1500 talents. The Delian League promoted inter-city commerce, standard measurements, a common coinage, and democracy.

In 454 BCE, Pericles moved the league's treasury to Athens, fearing the Persians would overcome Delos and steal the money. The other city-states suspected Pericles' true motive was to use the funds for his grandiose building projects in Athens – especially since members could no longer contribute ships, grain, or materials instead of money for their dues.

As Athens grew in power, its control over the Delian League transfigured it into the Athenian Empire. Athens had commanded naval operations from the beginning. When Pericles moved the treasury to Athens, this essentially turned Athens into an empire receiving tribute payments from more than 300 city-states. The once-equal allies were now subjects of Athens. Athens had little accountability for how the tribute money was spent. Athens now controlled all the city-states of mainland Greece – only Sparta and its Peloponnesian League allies were independent.

The Doric columns of the magnificent Parthenon stand today, 2500 years later!
https://commons.wikimedia.org/wiki/File:Parthenon_20180221-4.jpg

During the Greco-Persian wars, Athens had used the tribute from member states of the Delian League to build its powerful fleet and other expenses necessary to launch offensive strikes against the Persian-Achaemenid Empire. But now the wars were over, and the money was funding Pericles' ambitious building project on the Acropolis. And Athens could use its impressive fleet, funded by the other League members, to suppress any rebellious city-states – which it did! Resentment was growing in the city-states around the Aegean Sea and northern Greece.

As the threat of the Achaemenid Empire faded and tribute payments increased, some disgruntled city-states considered withdrawing from the Delian League. In 467 BCE, Naxos – the largest and wealthiest island in the Cyclades – tried to leave the alliance. Athens retaliated by removing Naxos' vote in the league, taking Naxos' naval vessels, and forcing the city to take down its defensive walls.

Another league member, the island of Thasos in the northern Aegean, felt its mines in Mount Pangaio were threatened when Athens set up a new colony – Amphipolis – on the Strymon River. Thasos withdrew from the league in 465 BCE. When Athens hit back, besieging the island, Thasos called on Sparta to help, but Sparta was too busy putting down its helot revolt. After two years, Athens' General Aristides accepted Thasos' surrender; the terms included forfeiting their naval ships, paying yearly fines, tearing down their defensive walls, and giving their mines to Athens.

Sparta and the rest of the Peloponnesian League were also at odds with Athens. After the Greeks chased the Persians away and the Athenians began rebuilding its twice-razed city, Sparta sent envoys to convince them not to rebuild their fortification walls. Of course, Athens said no! That would have made the city vulnerable to attack. Thucydides commented this made the Spartans feel aggrieved. Athens' suspicions about Sparta were well-founded. When Athens was laying siege to Thasos in 465 BCE, Sparta was secretly planning to attack the Attica peninsula. Suddenly, an earthquake that killed thousands was followed by a revolt of Sparta's helots (their semi-enslaved peasants), forcing Sparta to focus on internal affairs.

Sparta asked all its allies – including Athens – to help them get the helots under control. Athens sent 4000 hoplites to help suppress the uprising, but the Spartans inexplicably told them to go back home – while welcoming help from their other allies. This offended the Athenians to no end! Thucydides speculated that the Spartans felt the Athenians might have ulterior motives – secretly planning to support the helots.

When the Spartans and their allies finally forced the helots into submission, they felt it would be prudent to encourage them to evacuate Sparta, so they would no longer be a threat. Sparta's trust issues with Athens eroded further when Athens resettled the helots in Naupaktos – strategically located two miles directly across the Gulf of Corinth from the Peloponnese peninsula. In case of war between Athens and Sparta, Athens would have allies preventing enemies from sailing up the Gulf of Corinth to attack them.

Anticipating inevitable war with Sparta, Athens quickly negotiated strategic alliances: formidable Thessaly in northern Greece, Sparta's perennial enemy and neighbor Argos in the Peloponnese, and Sparta's former ally Megara on the Isthmus of Corinth. Megara was at war with powerful Corinth – also on the Isthmus of Corinth and a partner of Sparta. By allying with Megara, Athens got sucked into the fight against Corinth and her allies in the Peloponnese – which included Sparta; this conflict was the First Peloponnesian War, lasting from 460 to 445 BCE.

At the beginning of this war, Athens simultaneously sent a 200-ship naval fleet to help the Libyan King Inarus, who had stirred most of Egypt to revolt against Artaxerxes, king of Persia. Sending the ships to Africa strained resources for fighting the Peloponnesian League. Athens lost the land wars with Corinth and Epidaurus but scored a brilliant naval victory at the island of Cecryphaleia in the Saronic Gulf. This victory propelled another island in the gulf – Aegina – to enter the war, adding imposing naval forces to the Peloponnesian League's daunting fleet. Once again, Athens won a staggering victory – capturing 70 of the allied forces' ships.

To pull Athens away from Aegina, Corinth attacked Megara again. Rather than diverting the Athenian navy from the Saronic Gulf, a hodgepodge army of elderly Athenian men and young boys marched out to aid Megara. This dubious force managed to drive the Corinthians off – even entrapping and slaughtering a significant section of Corinth's army.

Sparta did not get especially involved at the beginning of this war and certainly not directly against Athens. A couple of years into the war, Sparta headed out to help Doris – their ancestral homeland – on the northern side of the Gulf of Corinth – against Doris' neighbor Phocis. Their mission was successful, but then Athens moved into the gulf – blocking their way home. So, Sparta marched around the bay to Boeotia – close to Athens! Athens' land army – not as invincible as its navy – marched out to meet them in the Battle of Tanagra, which Athens lost, although Sparta also suffered heavy losses. The Spartans decided not to invade Attica and marched home across the isthmus instead.

Athens bounced back from this loss to attack Boeotia, winning an outstanding triumph, gaining all of Boeotia except Thebes. Aegina surrendered soon after, joining the Delian League and paying tribute to Athens. Inspired by this victory, Athens' navy sailed around the Peloponnese, looting and sacking the coastal towns. With Athens' ally Megara guarding the isthmus and Athens' fleets in the Saronic and Corinthian gulfs, Athens was impregnable to attack from Sparta.

Flush with victory, Athens suffered an unexpected and appalling defeat by the Persians in Egypt – who decimated Athens' naval forces there. Athens lost interest in the Peloponnese, giving full attention to strengthening and organizing the Delian League against a Persian attack. Athens had to abandon Boeotia after suffering defeat at the Battle of Cornea, and no sooner did that happen than Megara and Euboea rebelled. These setbacks were reversed when Pericles attacked Euboea with 5000 men and 50 ships, squelching the revolt.

Soon after, the war ended when Sparta and Athens agreed to the Thirty-Year Peace, which gave Megara back to the Peloponnese and Aegina as Athens' tributary. But the peace would be short, lasting only half the promised thirty years.

Chapter 8: The Peloponnesian War

"Think, too, of the great part that is played by the unpredictable in war:

think of it now, before you are committed to war.

The longer a war lasts, the more things tend to depend on accidents . . .

And when people are entering upon a war, they do things the wrong way round.

Action comes first, and it is only when they have already suffered that they begin to think."

~Thucydides, *The Peloponnesian War*

From 431 to 404 BCE, the Peloponnesian War pitted Athens and the Athenian League against Sparta and the Peloponnesian League. Some historians call this the *second* Peloponnesian War, the first being the conflict from 460 to 445 BCE. The Peloponnesian War was a massive showdown between Athens' superior naval force and Sparta's infantry war machine.

Despite having agreed to the Thirty-Year Peace, hostilities between Athens and Sparta soon resumed. Once again, Corinth was an audacious agitator. At odds with its colony of Corcyra, Corinth began to put together a navy with its Peloponnesian allies. Corcyra pleaded for help from the Athenians, who sent a small fleet to defend Corcyra from Corinth – with instructions only to safeguard, *not* launch an offensive against the Corinthian fleet – since that would break the Thirty-Year Peace. Did they follow instructions? No – they did not! The Athenian fleet would have suffered a crushing defeat if more triremes from Athens had not arrived just in time.

This reconstruction shows how a Greek naval fleet may have looked.

Imagine a fleet of 80 or more of these ships!
https://commons.wikimedia.org/wiki/File:Greek_Galleys.jpg

Athens and Corinth clashed again regarding the matter of Potidaea – a Corinthian colony in northern Greece that had joined the Delian League. Athens didn't like Potidaea having Corinthian magistrates – so they ordered the city-state to get rid of them. The Athenians' high-handedness outraged the Corinthians, who promised to support Potidaea in a revolt from Athens. When Potidaea revolted, Corinth clandestinely sent men to help fight Athens.

Corinth ran to Sparta asking for aid against Athens, and then an Athenian delegation gate-crashed the Spartan assembly. The Corinthians jeered at Sparta for its passivity – saying if they didn't act soon, they'd be surrounded by Athenians and without allies. The Athenians asked the Spartans if they really wanted to challenge their indomitable naval force and break the Thirty-Year Peace. The Spartans determined Athens had already broken the peace treaty, and thus war was now on the table.

For seven years, beginning in 431 BCE, Athens butted heads with Megara, a Spartan ally on the coast between Athens and the Peloponnese, across from Salamis. Athens set up a fort on Salamis and blockaded ships carrying supplies and grain to Megara – causing severe food shortages. The Megarian and Peloponnesian naval forces attacked the Salamis fort in 429 BCE, but Athens' watchmen noticed their beacon lights, and Athens sailed a fleet over, routing the Megarian-Peloponnesian fleets.

In 427 BCE, Megara kicked out their oligarchy and embraced democracy for a few months until the exiled aristocracy mustered their forces and retook the city. However, the democratic faction in Megara wanted to ally with democratic Athens, so the Megarian oligarchy called on Sparta for help. While the Megarians holed up inside the city, Sparta and Athens fought just outside their walls, until finally, the outnumbered Athenians backed down, and Megara opened its gates to Sparta.

While fighting Megara, Athens engaged in the Archidamian War (named after Spartan King Archidamus II) from 431 to 421 – the Peloponnesian War's first phase. Sparta's warriors stripped the fields bare around Athens, trying to provoke a pitched battle.

Pericles stopped the people from suicidal attacks on the Spartan raiders – knowing the Spartans had the upper hand in land battles.

The rural people poured inside Athens' defensive walls, and Pericles ordered regular grain shipments from Athens' eastern colonies to feed the population. Meanwhile, Athens' stellar navy blocked sea access to the Peloponnesian peninsula, cutting off food and supplies to Sparta and its allies.

Athens had enough food shipments to feed everyone, but Pericles never imagined the plague that came with the cargo from Egypt – perhaps carried by rats in the grain. Thucydides, the historian – who got the plague and recovered – described the symptoms as beginning with fever, headache, and inflamed eyes, followed by a bleeding throat and tongue, sneezing, chest congestion, coughing, vomiting, and violent spasms. The skin was red, with small bumps breaking out.

Some survivors lost their eyesight, fingers, toes, or private parts from tissue death. Some lost their memory. Death came to one-third of the city – usually on the sixth or seventh day of the illness, with violent diarrhea. Bodies of the dead were cast into colossal mass graves or burned on pyres. Archeologists found one pit of 240 skeletons – all buried in one day. Some died alone in their houses, with no one to bury them – their rotting bodies filling the city with stench.

The Athenians felt the gods must have abandoned them in favor of Sparta, but Thucydides – historian and military general – applied Hippocrates' direct observation method. He noted the vultures avoided eating the plague victims lying about; if they did, the birds died after eating the corpses. He also observed that no one who got it and survived was infected again. In his day, the understanding of contagious pathogens was just beginning to evolve.

How could Athens fight Sparta and the other Peloponnesians with their military men sick or dead from the plague? They couldn't even hire mercenaries. On the bright side, Sparta was afraid to come anywhere near Athens and was no longer pillaging their fields. Ironically, Athens had unintentionally protected Sparta and the Peloponnese from the plague by blockading shipments into the peninsula – ships that carried the plague. So long as they stayed on the Peloponnese – they were safe!

In 429 BCE, Pericles was inconsolable when both his sons died from the plague. Then he became ill and died not long after. The plague's decimation of Athens' population cost the city greatly in the war with Sparta. Even worse was the loss of Pericles, as his inferior successors lacked his keen insight and leadership skills. Athens' splendor and renown were beginning to flicker.

Despite losing Pericles and one-third of their population, Athens slowly revived – picking up again with naval raids on coastal towns of the Peloponnese and building their own fortified posts around the peninsula. One post on the tiny island of Sphacteria was Pylos, which began attracting helot runaways. The Spartans feared their helot serfs would revolt again – with Athens' encouragement. Sparta attacked the Athenian fort of Pylos, but the Athenians unexpectedly won the Battle of Sphacteria when they managed to surround 300 Spartan hoplites – who surrendered! This unpredicted victory emboldened the Athenians – the Spartans' land army wasn't invincible after all!

After this, General Brasidas of Sparta marched through northern Greece to Amphipolis – Athens' colony in Thrace that controlled the silver mines supplying Athens' war funding. General Thucydides hurried to Thrace with an Athenian force, but Sparta had already taken Amphipolis. Athens exiled Thucydides for arriving too late! However, in the ensuing Battle of Amphipolis, both Sparta's general Brasidas and Athens' general Cleon died – leading the two cities to agree to the Peace of Nicias.

The 50-year Peace of Nicias restored most territories to where they were before the war, released prisoners-of-war, and Athens agreed to help Sparta if the helots revolted again. However, most of Sparta's allies refused to sign the treaty.

The 50-year Peace of Nicias lasted only six years. Some of Sparta's Peloponnese allies were restless under Sparta's control. They allied with powerful Argos – that had never joined Sparta's league –forming their own coalition with Athens' encouragement. Sparta felt gravely threatened when the alliance attacked the nearby city of Tegea. The biggest Peloponnesian War land battle raged at the Battle of Mantinea, with the Spartans and Tegeans facing off against the new Argive coalition and a small Athenian force. Sparta overwhelmingly triumphed, forcing the rebel states back into the Peloponnesian League.

The young, handsome, and charismatic General Alcibiades, known for unconventional battle tactics, was a rising star in Athens. Socrates instructed him as a youth; they shared a close relationship. After he signed the Peace of Nicias, it wasn't long before Alcibiades began stirring up trouble with Sparta by conning Sparta's ambassadors – who had come to Athens to work out the particulars of the Nicias treaty – to embarrass the treaty's negotiator Nicias, enabling Alcibiades to grab power. Once he gained control, he aligned with Argos and the rebel Peloponnesians, setting his sights on Syracuse – the fabulously wealthy Sicilian city that controlled the lion's share of Mediterranean trade – and was allied with Sparta.

The small city of Segesta belonged to the indigenous people who lived in Sicily long before the Ionians (related to the Athenians) and the Dorians (related to the Spartans) arrived. Now Segesta was at war with Selinus – a Dorian Greek city friendly with Syracuse (and, by extension, Sparta). In 415 BCE, Segesta asked Athens to help them fight Selinus. Athens had been looking for an excuse to go to war with Syracuse, and by fighting Selinus, they knew Syracuse would get involved. They told Segesta they would help, beginning the second wave of the Peloponnesian War – the Sicily Expedition.

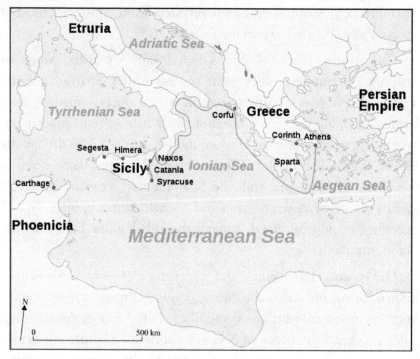

This map shows the Athenian fleet's route to Sicily – hugging the land, as the triremes were not suited for the high seas.

By Morn - Own work, CC BY-SA 4.0.
*h*ttps://commons.wikimedia.org/w/index.php?curid=100326670

Athens' magnificent fleet sailed out from Piraeus with 284 ships, 5100 hoplites, 700 slingers, 480 archers, and 30 cavalrymen and their horses. Nearing the coast of Sicily, the three generals – Alcibiades, Nicias, and Lamachus – discussed their next move.

Nicias wanted to settle affairs between Segesta and Selinus, sail around the island to impress the Sicilians with their stunning fleet, then head home. Alcibiades thought Nicias' plan was a disgrace – he wanted to drum up support against Syracuse from other Ionian-Greek cities. The elderly Lamachus thought both plans were idiotic. "Syracuse doesn't know we're coming! We need to sail directly to Syracuse and attack when they are unprepared!"

But the other two disagreed, and Alcibiades' plan won out – unfortunately. It turned out that the Ionian Sicilians weren't enthusiastic about attacking Syracuse. Then, in an unexpected turn of events, Athens sent a ship to Sicily to take Alcibiades back to Athens on charges of sacrilege and conspiracy. Knowing his political enemies trumped up the charges – and that he had little chances in Athens – Alcibiades went with them but escaped when the ship stopped off in Italy. Guess where he went? To Sparta! He'd turned traitor! Now he could advise Sparta of Athens' strategies and strengths.

Meanwhile, the weird battle of the walls began in Sicily. Declaring Athens had breached the Peace of Nicias, Sparta sent its navy to Syracuse. To choke off Syracuse, the Athenians began building a wall extending from the sea to the harbor. The Syracusans at once began building walls from the city going out – to cut through where the Athenian barricade was to go. Each side raided the other to disrupt the wall-building.

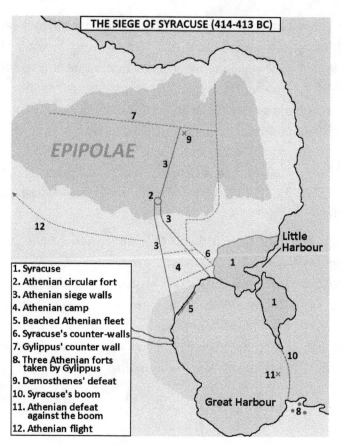

THE SIEGE OF SYRACUSE (414-413 BC)

EPIPOLAE

7

9

3

2

12

3

3

6

Little
Harbour

4

1

1

5

10

11

8

Great Harbour

1. Syracuse
2. Athenian circular fort
3. Athenian siege walls
4. Athenian camp
5. Beached Athenian fleet
6. Syracuse's counter-walls
7. Gylippus' counter wall
8. Three Athenian forts taken by Gylippus
9. Demosthenes' defeat
10. Syracuse's boom
11. Athenian defeat against the boom
12. Athenian flight

This map depicts the war of the walls in the siege of Syracuse.

By T8612 - Own work, CC BY-SA 4.0.
https://commons.wikimedia.org/w/index.php?curid=101154856

In round one, the Athenians destroyed Syracuse's counter-wall. Athens demolished Syracuse's second wall, but the Syracusans killed General Lamachus in the fray, leaving the cautious Nicias as the only general. Nicias dithered while the Spartan fleet approached Syracuse, and he didn't finish the walls surrounding Syracuse in time. The Peloponnesian fleet landed, and General Gylippus marched onshore with 2700 men – just as the Syracusans were about to surrender to Athens! With renewed vigor, the Syracusans built a new wall, this time successfully blocking the Athenian attempt to hem them in, winning the war of the walls.

After this debacle, Nicias transitioned to naval offensives. But the usually indomitable Athenian navy met its match with the Syracusan and Corinthian fleets. Despite the hopelessness of the situation, Nicias inexplicably pressed on. As a tidal wave of Peloponnesian reinforcements sailed toward Sicily, Nicias finally decided to leave – but just then, a lunar eclipse convinced him to remain another month – a fatal mistake.

Syracuse entrapped the Athenian navy with a line of ships sealing the harbor. The Athenians' last-ditch attempt to breach the wall of vessels ended in a tangle of colliding ships. Onshore, the Athenian land army despaired, watching as their ships sunk, one by one. They tried to retreat, but the Syracusans cut off their escape routes. Nicias' attempt to bribe the Syracusans was met with laughter and a shower of arrows. The Syracusans and Spartans massacred most of the Athenians, including Nicias, sold Athens' allies into slavery, and left the captured Athenians in a stone quarry to starve.

Sparta declared victory in Sicily and took the war to Athens in the Peloponnesian War's third wave: the Decelean or Ionian War. Following the traitorous Alcibiades' advice, Sparta took control of the city of Decelea, preventing overland trade to Athens. Worse yet, Sparta took Athens' silver mines, cutting off Athens' income and forcing Athens to require higher tribute payments from its allies – escalating tension and leading to most of Ionia revolting against Athens.

Syracuse sent their fleet to aid Sparta, and the Persians got involved when Sparta commissioned them to build warships. Not only was Athens facing an ominous external crisis, but a revolution erupted with a 400-man oligarchy seizing power, squelching Athens' democracy. On Samos, Athens' fleet refused to answer to the new government and appointed Alcibiades as their new general. Yes – Alcibiades! Once again, he switched sides – things were getting a little hot for him over in Sparta when King Agis suspected Alcibiades was sleeping with his queen.

In 410 BCE, Alcibiades led the renegade Athenian fleet to the Hellespont in the Battle of Cyzicus against Sparta, Persia, and Syracuse's joint forces, decimating the Spartan and Syracusan fleets. This astounding victory prompted the Athenians to overthrow their oligarchy, restore democracy, and regain their tributary cities in Ionia - helping them financially. But trouble loomed on the horizon: with Persian funding, the Spartans were rebuilding their fleet.

Not only was the Persian-Achaemenid emperor Darius II allying with and supporting Sparta, but Darius also reconquered most of Ionia. His second son, Cyrus the Younger, partnered with Sparta's General Lysander - each hoping to become absolute rulers of their respective realms. Just after his father Darius II died, Cyrus put his revenues from his Asia Minor cities at Lysander's disposal in return for Lysander's support of his planned overthrow of his older brother, Artaxerxes II - Persia's new emperor. Cyrus would die in his attempt to usurp his brother, but that would be in 401 BCE - now, he was aiding Lysander to victory.

In Athens, Alcibiades got voted out as general after his failed strategy in the Battle of Notium against Sparta's General Lysander in Ephesus. Disgraced, Alcibiades left Athens, never to return.

Athens scored an unexpected victory in the Battle of Arginusae, sinking 70 Spartan ships using novel and unusual tactics. It turned out to be their last naval victory. A fierce storm prevented them from rescuing their crews from their damaged ships or destroying the rest of Sparta's fleet. Athens held a trial and executed six Athenian generals for dereliction of duty - leaving an Athenian navy without experienced leadership.

Lysander's next move was to sail to the Dardanelles, cutting off Athens' grain shipments. Athens sent their demoralized navy to confront the Spartans, but the Battle of Aegospotami ended in horrendous defeat for the Athenians - 168 of their 180 ships sank, and the Spartans captured 4000 sailors.

The war was over. In 404 BCE, Athens and its allies sued for peace, forced to demolish their own city walls, hand over their naval fleet, and surrender their tributary cities. Although Corinth and Thebes wanted to enslave the Athenians, Sparta remembered how they had saved all of Greece from the Persians and allowed the city to stand and the people to remain free.

Chapter 9: From Sparta to Thebes

"The keenest sorrow is to recognize ourselves as the sole cause of all our adversities."

~Sophocles

After crushing Athens, Sparta replaced Athens' hegemony, inserting its garrisons and governors throughout the other Greek states, even imposing oligarchies on earlier democracies. Once Sparta's great ally, Thebes now experienced Sparta's dark side: forced to dismantle its Boeotian League, become an oligarchy, and endure Sparta's garrison on the Cadmea - its citadel. Helplessly, the citizens watched as Sparta exiled or executed any critics. "This won't last forever," they breathed. "One day, we will overcome."

General Lysander set up pro-Spartan governments in city-states around the Aegean Sea with *decarchies* (oligarchies of ten men) led by *harmosts* (Spartan military governors). Lysander appointed leadership loyal to him - not necessarily to Sparta - essentially creating his private empire. Athens' instability between democratic and oligarchic factions gave Lysander the excuse to interfere, appointing the "Thirty Tyrants" oligarchy - a puppet government loyal to him.

However, Athens' exiled general Thrasybulus led a successful democratic revolution against Lysander's oligarchy, killing the leader of the Thirty Tyrants, then fighting Lysander's Spartan force. Although Athens lost, and despite Lysander's protests, King Pausanias of Sparta allowed a democratic government to resume in Athens. The Spartan co-rulers – King Pausanias and King Agis – were increasingly concerned about Lysander's unbridled power; they also ended the forced oligarchies in the Greek city-states.

When King Agis died in 401 BCE, his brother Agesilaus II succeeded him because the legitimacy of Agis' son Leotychidas was uncertain – rumors floated that Leotychidas was the love-child from Alcibiades' affair with Queen Timaea after he defected to Sparta. Agesilaus was born lame: it's a wonder he survived infancy, as Spartans usually left any weak or defective babies on a mountain to die. When Agesilaus was a boy, Lysander had been his *erastes* (adult sexual partner) in a pederasty relationship. Lysander hoped his influence over Agesilaus would restore his power.

During the Peloponnesian War, Sparta gave Persia the overlordship of Asia Minor's Greek city-states. However, because Sparta had supported Cyrus the Younger's unsuccessful attempt to usurp King Artaxerxes II's throne, it now faced the Persian emperor's wrath. Sparta was stirring up Asia Minor's Greek city-states against the Persian satrap (governor). Lysander and Agesilaus formed an army of 2000 freed helots, 30 Spartan warriors, and 6000 Greek allies to fight Persia.

When they reached Ephesus, Lysander was in his element, renewing old acquaintances with men he'd appointed to leadership and overshadowing King Agesilaus. Resenting his patronizing ways, the young king kept Lysander in Asia Minor – isolated from Sparta. After a stunning victory at the Battle of Sardis, Agesilaus received command of both the army and naval forces – he delegated the navy to Peisander, his brother-in-law.

The Persian satrap Tithraustes bribed the Greek city-states to fight Sparta and paid for rebuilding Athens' walls.

https://commons.wikimedia.org/wiki/File:CUH_Agesilaus_and_Pharnabazus.jpg

Thebes and Corinth – Sparta's one-time allies – were disgruntled with the Peloponnesian war settlement and Sparta's browbeating leadership and imperialistic takeovers of smaller city-states. Tithraustes, the Persian satrap of Sardis, bribed Sparta's former allies to fight back. Pharnabazus, the Persian satrap of Phrygia, visited Greece around 396 BCE, also bribing the Greek city-states to war against Sparta, thus beginning the Corinthian War (395 – 387 BCE).

Thebes led the way by stirring up war between two small city-states on the Gulf of Corinth: Ozolian Locris, a Spartan ally, and Phocis, a Theban partner. Just as the Thebans predicted, Sparta jumped headlong into the conflict, defending Locris while Thebes backed Phocis, aided by Athens, Thebes' newest ally.

The Spartans sent two armies – one led by King Pausanias and the other by Lysander (recalled from Asia). Lysander was to gather allies from northwestern Greece and rendezvous with Pausanias on the southern Greece mainland to attack Haliartus – a sister city of Thebes. Lysander got there first, and without waiting for Pausanias, he besieged Haliartus.

Lysander didn't realize a Theban army was in the region, and they counterattacked Lysander's forces under Haliartus' walls, killing Lysander and routing his army. But the Thebans pursued the Spartans too far. Putting a favorite tactic into play, the Spartans suddenly whirled around and attacked the Thebans, catching them off-guard and killing a large section of their army.

Pausanias finally arrived a couple of days later, asking Thebes for a truce so he could recover the bodies of Lysander and the other fallen Spartans. The Thebans gave permission but required the Spartans to abandon Boeotia. When King Pausanias returned to Sparta, Lysanders' supporters took him to trial for arriving late at Haliartus and not attacking the city when he did come. Pausanias went into exile, leaving his underage son Agesipolis to co-reign with King Agesilaus.

Sparta's defeat at Haliartus encouraged other aggrieved city-states to join forces with Thebes: Argos, Corinth, and most cities in central and northern Greece. The Spartans recalled King Agesilaus from Asia Minor. While King Agesilaus was returning by land in 394 BCE, the Spartan fleet of 85 triremes under Commander Peisander sailed out from Cnidus (Knidos) in southwestern Asia Minor, also returning to Greece.

But two enemy fleets confronted the Spartan fleet: a Persian-Achaemenid force commanded by the Athenian Conon and a Phoenician fleet commanded by Pharnabazus, the Persian satrap. Overwhelmed, the Spartans bolted, beaching most of their fleet and fleeing inland. The Persian-Phoenician-Athenian coalition captured 50 Spartan triremes and killed Peisander and many of his marines.

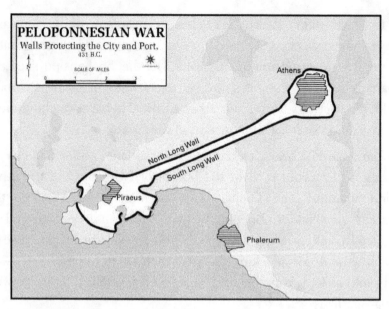

Athens' long walls surrounded the city, then extended to the port of Piraeus. By U.S. Army Cartographer Public Domain, https://commons.wikimedia.org/w/index.php?curid=1604331

This debacle ended Sparta's naval empire, and Athens soon reclaimed dominance over the seas. Conon continued with his fleet, raiding the Peloponnese coast with Persia's satrap Pharnabazus, then returned to Athens to rebuild Athens' long walls, paid for by Pharnabazus. The walls surrounded the city, then extended seven miles to encompass the port of Piraeus, supplying safe passage from Athens to its harbor.

As King Agesilaus' men entered Boeotia on their march back to Sparta, they met a coalition force of Argives, Athenians, Corinthians, Thebans, and other allies – 20,000 hoplites to Agesilaus' 15,000. A partial solar eclipse they'd seen days earlier unnerved Agesilaus' men. King Agesilaus kept the news of the traumatic naval defeat at Cnidus a secret from his regiment, not wanting to rattle them further.

In the ensuing Battle of Coronea, both armies approached each other in silence – unusual because the Spartans normally marched to pipes and battle chants. When they were 660 feet out, the Thebans suddenly charged headlong, shrieking their war cry. When they were halfway across the field, the Spartans suddenly broke into a run – once again, unusual because they usually marched steadily up to the lines. Even before the Spartans reached them, the Argives panicked and raced for the hills.

However, on the other flank, the Thebans broke through Sparta's allies and were ransacking the Spartan's baggage. Wheeling his phalanx around, Agesilaus charged the Thebans, just as the Thebans looked up to see the Argives racing in retreat up Mount Helicon. Instead of facing the Spartans in phalanx formation or running *away*, they desperately tried to break through the Spartan phalanx to get back to the rest of the army at Mount Helicon. Of course, that was suicidal – 600 Thebans and their allies died in the bloodbath.

The Corinthian War ended in 387 BCE with the King's Peace or Peace of Antalcidas – named after the Spartan diplomat who negotiated it, influenced and guaranteed by Persia's King Artaxerxes II. The Spartan Commander Antalcidas, whose 90-trireme fleet guarded the Hellespont, blocking Athens' grain shipments from the Black Sea, forced the Athenians to the negotiating table. Wary of fighting without Athens' support, Argos, Corinth, and Thebes joined the treaty.

This bronze sculpture depicts a Spartan "banqueter," although the young Spartan men usually ate black bean soup in their barracks. Simplicity and discipline were essential Spartan virtues.

https://commons.wikimedia.org/wiki/File:Bronze_banqueter_from_the_tripod_su pport_of_a_bronze_bowl_Laconian_530- 500_BCE_from_Dodona_British_Museum.jpg

Artaxerxes' terms included Persian possession of the Greek city-states in Asia Minor, along with Cyprus. All other Greek city-states would be autonomous, except Lemnos, Imbros, and Scyros still belonging to Athens – as they had from ancient times. Anyone who broke the truce would face Artaxerxes' wrath. Sparta's Peloponnesian league was the only union that remained, and the Persian king put Sparta in charge of enforcing the peace.

Athens had learned from its past mistakes and Sparta's blunders. After General Thrasybulus restored democracy to Athens in 403 BCE, the city not only survived but thrived throughout the next century – gradually regaining significant power. In 378 BCE, the Athenians created the Second Athenian League. Instead of coercing membership, Athens now used finesse to attract city-states to join a decentralized alliance where everyone would keep their local autonomy.

General Thrasybulus sailed around the Aegean in 394 BCE, visiting city-states formerly belonging to the Athenian Alliance, aiding with democratic revolutions but otherwise keeping out of their internal affairs. These low-key, amiable actions broke Spartan influence and formed governments friendly to Athens – without needing Athenian garrisons. Now, the city-states perceived Athens as their liberator from Spartan oppression.

Athens was the head of the new league, but every member state got an equal vote – except Athens, who had no vote! Athens was the horse that pulled the carriage, while the city-states held the reins – at least, for the time being. In a sincere effort to correct the first Athenian League's abuses, Athens now had no power over the other members in the new league, which endured until 338 BCE, when the Hellenic League replaced it.

Despite the King's Peace, Sparta seized Thebes' citadel in 382 BCE, trying to reestablish hegemony and squelch Thebe's growing power. General Pelopidas and other leading statemen fled to Athens, where they regrouped and plotted their comeback. Meanwhile, in Thebes, Pelopidas' close friend Epaminondas was secretly preparing the young men led by Gorgidas to fight the interlopers.

In 379 BCE, Pelopidas snuck back into Thebes with a dozen other exiles. Joining with Gorgidas' men, they assassinated the Spartan-appointed government leaders and surrounded the Spartan garrison on Cadmea, the citadel. The next day, the Theban assembly declared Pelopidas, Epaminondas, and Gorgidas as their liberators. Under attack by the entire city, the Spartan garrison surrendered, allowed to leave the city unharmed.

Their defeat of Spartan supremacy – thought to be indestructible – psychologically empowered the Thebans, and they quickly reformed the Boeotian League. The coup d'état instigated a war between Sparta and Thebes, with Sparta invading Boeotia three times in the next seven years. Thebes fought back with guerrilla tactics, mostly avoiding face-to-face battles. Gorgidas formed the Sacred Band with 300 full-time warriors, spending most of their time training with weapons, tactics, wrestling, and equestrian skills.

The final collapse of Spartan hegemony took place at the sensational 371 BCE Battle of Leuctra. King Cleombrotus I led the Spartans and their Peloponnesian allies toward Thebes, but a Theban force blocked the way. Cleombrotus circled around them, then over the mountains, storming Creusis on the Gulf of Corinth, capturing 12 Theban warships, then quickly marched north, catching Thebes by surprise.

Epaminondas and the Boeotian League rushed south to meet the Spartan coalition near Leuctra, only seven miles from Thebes! Sparta had 9000 hoplites, 1000 peltast infantry (more lightly armed than the hoplites), and 1000 cavalry. The Boeotian League faced off with 6000 hoplites, 1000 peltasts, and 1500 cavalry.

On the night before the battle, a ghost came to Pelopidas in a dream, demanding he sacrifice a red-haired virgin to ensure triumph over Sparta. Troubled, he consulted his divinators, who disagreed on whether they should engage in human sacrifice. Just then, a chestnut-colored filly galloped through the camp and suddenly reared and stopped right in front of them. This must be the red-haired virgin! Relieved, they sacrificed the horse.

Just before the battle, Epaminondas saw a large snake, and with his troops watching, crushed its head. "The body is useless without the head! If we crush Sparta, its allies will likewise be useless!"

The Theban's left phalanx formation was 50-men deep, while Sparta's entire phalanx was only 12 men deep – although deeper than usual for Spartan warriors. When the battle began, Sparta initially held their line until the Thebans killed King Cleombrotus – then the Spartans began to break up and soon abruptly spun around in retreat. At least 1000 Spartans died, compared to 300 Thebans. Thebes had crushed the snake's head.

Thebes stunning and unexpected victory over Sparta at Leuctra lifted Thebes as the new Greek hegemony for a decade. The Spartans had subdued Athens, and now the Spartans were subdued by the Corinthian War, the defeat at Leuctra – and primarily by running out of men to send to war. The birth rate was low because young Spartan men lived in the barracks, not with their wives, and were often away at war. Newborn babies were abandoned to die if they didn't measure up to inspection. The Spartan men who did grow up continually died on the battlefield.

Meanwhile, Thebes' oligarchy leaders – Pelopidas and Epaminondas – were on a roll, winning battles through innovative tactics: spearmen in creative phalanx formation and with longer spears. Thebes began to expand their influence beyond the Boeotian League. They sent forces into the Peloponnese, rescuing the Arcadians and Messenians from Spartan domination and setting up an Arcadian League friendly to Thebes. In an invasion of Thessaly, they captured a young Philip II of Macedon and brought him to Thebes – little knowing how the tables would soon turn for him. Another battle in Thessaly in 364 BCE was successful, but Pelopidas died there through his recklessness in charging the enemy.

The Spartans allied with the Eleans, who were trying to sabotage the Arcadian League. But the Arcadians sabotaged themselves by seizing Zeus' sanctuary of Olympia in Elis, compelling one of their member city-states, Mantinea, to abandon the league. Sparta jumped on that opportunity, inviting the Mantineans to join them and the Eleans in an assault on the Arcadian League.

Surprisingly, Athens threw its lot in with Sparta, nervous about Thebes' strengthening hegemony and remembering how Sparta had spared their city at the Peloponnesian War's end – when Thebes and Corinth howled for their destruction. The Athenians sent their forces to Sparta by sea – to avoid passing through territory controlled by Thebes' allies.

Epaminondas marched his Theban army into the Peloponnese, meeting up with the Arcadian League. In 362 BCE, the Theban-Arcadian coalition faced off against the Spartans, Eleans, Mantineans, and Athenians – led by King Agesilaus II – near Mantinea. As he had at Leuctra, Epaminondas organized his hoplites into a deep phalanx, leading from the front line himself. Rather than a straight line, the phalanx was a wedge shape – like a ship's bow plowing through the water.

Thebes started well, eliminating their opponents' cavalry and performing a swift turn with their phalanx to push into the enemy's right phalanx, crashing into the Mantineans' lines and killing the Mantinean General Podares. But then a spear struck Epaminondas in his chest. His warriors carried him off the battlefield, still alive, but barely. His protégées and planned successors Iolaidas and Daiphantus died soon after. Although Thebes won the battle, in his last words, Epaminondas instructed the Thebes to make peace, knowing that without seasoned leadership, Thebes could not maintain a hegemony.

Now Thebes, even though gradually weakening, invaded Sparta's territories, freeing their helots, which led to Sparta's ultimate collapse. Thebes permanently smashed Spartan's hegemony at Leuctra. Sparta could not sustain a full-time citizen army without their workers and could never again gain the upper hand.

On the other hand, Thebes overreached – trying to control both northern and southern Greece. Thebes had also lost the two brilliant leaders – Pelopidas and Epaminondas – who had spurred their rising hegemony. Without them, they could not perpetuate their dominance. With neither Sparta nor Thebes dominating, the door was open to a newcomer – Philip of Macedon. Yes! That Philip, the one Thebes had once held hostage. Now Macedon would rise to conquer and lead Greece in an unimaginable empire-building endeavor.

Chapter 10: Classical Art and Philosophy

"Events will take their course; it is no good being angry at them.

He is happiest who wisely turns them to the best account."

~Euripides

Although political strife and wars for hegemony marked Greece's Classical Age, it was also a time of incredible cultural growth pervading the Greek world and extending to other civilizations – notably Rome. Art, literature, philosophy, and science surged to unprecedented heights. Greece's cultural, mathematical, and scientific achievements of its Classical Age have inspired and impacted civilizations for the past 2500 years.

Classical Greece is renowned for its unique architectural style; the remnants of breathtaking temples display its elegant columns and other structures reflecting harmony, symmetry, and intricate detail. The Temple of Apollo Epicurus at Bassae in the Peloponnese combined all three Greek architectural orders: Doric, Ionic, and Corinthian. Its architect, Ictinus – who also built Athens' Parthenon m- introduced innovative features, such as 15 columns (instead of 13) on its long sides and an inner-sanctum column positioned to reflect the sun.

The graceful Temple of Poseidon stands regally over the sea.
https://commons.wikimedia.org/wiki/File:Temple_de_posido.JPG

The Temple of the sea god Poseidon at Cape Sounion overlooks the Mediterranean from a high bluff at the tip of the Attica Peninsula – seen by those sailing to and from Athens. It has a traditional layout with 20-foot-tall Doric columns of marble.

Classical Greece's graceful, fluid, and natural sculptures expressed energetic, exuberant movement in dynamic poses. The colossal 41-foot-tall statue of the god Zeus stood in the temple of Zeus at Olympia – crafted by Phidias with gold and ivory plates covering a wooden frame. One of the Seven Wonders of the Ancient World, a fire destroyed it in 425 CE.

This reproduction of the Athena Parthenos' colossal statue in Nashville's Centennial Park is a full-scale replica of the Parthenon.

https://commons.wikimedia.org/wiki/File:Athena_Parthenos_LeQuire.jpg

Phidias also sculpted the 38-foot-high statue of Athena for the Parthenon in Athens, also on a wooden frame covered by gold sheets with ivory face and arms. The tyrant Lachares used the gold sheets to pay his army in 296 BCE, replacing them with copper. Fire destroyed the statue in 165 BCE. Descriptions written about the Zeus and Athena statues and images on coins give us an idea of how they looked.

The endearing marble sculpture of Hermes of Praxiteles was unearthed in 1877 at the Temple of Hera in Olympia – the temple had collapsed in an earthquake, burying the statue for 2000 years. Hermes is holding the baby Dionysus. Traces of cinnabar – a mercury sulfate – indicate he had tinted hair.

A stunning, well-preserved bronze sculpture recovered from an ancient shipwreck in the sea off Cape Artemision in Euboea probably represents either Zeus or Poseidon. He stands poised to throw something in his raised arm – probably a thunderbolt or trident, depending on which god he was.

Is he Zeus or Poseidon?

Photo by Ricardo André Frantz (User:Tetraktys) - Own work, CC BY-SA 3.0
https://commons.wikimedia.org/w/index.php?curid=2442534

Archeologists excavated the Kritios Boy sculpture from Athens' Acropolis. He stands in the relaxed *Contrapposto* poise, which became popular in Classical Greece – with most of his weight on one foot. His skin, bones, and muscles are sculpted with lifelike accuracy – a Classical era innovation.

Classical-era Greeks loved dramatic performances – especially tragedies, which portrayed themes of betrayal, unrequited or lost love, the impact of heedless immorality or crime, and the chaotic relationships between the gods and men. Aristotle felt that watching tragedy performances led to *catharsis* or purging of strong emotions.

The three most famous tragedy playwrights were Aeschylus, Euripides, and Sophocles. The "Father of Tragedy," Aeschylus wrote as many as 80 tragedies, but only seven survive today. His *Oresteia* was a trilogy of *Agamemnon, Libation Bearers,* and *Eumenides* – portraying the Argos royal family's bloody chain of revenge and murder.

Euripides was appreciated more in the generations after he died than in his lifetime. He innovated *tragicomedies* – tragedy with comic twists – and often used Greek myths for his subject matter. One of his tragedies was *Helen*, where she gives her side of the story in the events leading up to the Trojan War.

Greek drama used few actors -- one actor would portray several characters by changing masks like this one. Male actors played both male and female parts.

https://commons.wikimedia.org/wiki/File:Greek_tragedy_mask,_4th_cent._B.C._ (PAM_4640,_1-6-2020).jpg

Sophocles was the most popular of the three masters of tragedy. Seven of his plays endured to the present day, the most famous is *Oedipus Rex* – the tragic tale of the Theban king who killed his father and married his mother without knowing who they were.

Dramatic comedies were mostly satires using slapstick humor, dirty jokes, and bawdy costumes. Aristophanes was the master comic playwright. In his play, *The Frogs*, the contemporary Greek playwrights are terrible writers, so the protagonist, Dionysus, goes to Hades to bring Euripides back from the dead, to show the playwrights how it's done.

Classical Greek philosophers contemplated ethics and political affairs and discussed their theories on human nature and moral dilemmas. The Sophists weren't especially interested in the rightness of ethics or politics – their passion lay in eloquently presenting their side so well they convinced their audience. They would argue that evil is good, up is down, and other ridiculous themes - just for the sake of winning an argument.

Protagoras taught that all truth is relative, and everyone has their own truth - no one can ever say something is absolutely right or wrong. Any issue has two sides - one could convincingly defend either side - and he loved nothing more than taking the "weaker" side and supporting it with brilliant arguments! He was an agnostic, saying he was in no position to know whether the gods existed or what they looked like.

The Sophist philosopher Gorgias taught that nothing exists. Well, it might exist, but we can't know that it exists. Even if we know something exists, we can't communicate its existence. He used a pervasively ironic oratory style and often contradicted his own statements - for him, the subject of an argument was inconsequential; it was how one masterfully argued it.

Hippias, another Sophist, was a true renaissance man - specializing in astronomy, history, mathematics, music, art, and philosophy. In geometry, he discovered the quadratrix - a curve used to trisect an angle. In philosophy, he taught that a universal and changeless natural law is the foundation of morality. Right and wrong should not be decided by society's changing and arbitrary whims but by what is intrinsically good or evil in all places and times.

The most renowned philosophers of all time were Socrates, Plato, and Aristotle. Aristotle was the student of Plato, who was the student and dear friend of Socrates. Socrates apparently authored no books - Plato's writings preserved his teachings, along with Xenophon and Aristophanes.

Jacques-Louis David's The Death of Socrates depicts the philosopher's execution.

https://commons.wikimedia.org/wiki/File:David_-_The_Death_of_Socrates.jpg

Socrates never wanted to tell anyone what to think – he wanted his students to think for themselves. To that end, he employed a question-and-answer teaching method and claimed that he was absent of knowledge. He compared his "simple" ignorance – his awareness that he didn't have all the answers – to the "double" ignorance of clueless people – ignorant that they were unaware, yet insisting they had all the answers.

Socrates said the unexamined life is not worth living. If we don't think – we are little more than animals. Thus, he constantly interrogated the commonly held opinions of his fellow Athenians. He said he was a gadfly irritating the horse (Athens); through challenging them to philosophical inquiry, he was stirring up their stagnant sluggishness and complacency – the enemy of democracy.

Plato taught the *Theory of Forms* – what we see is not reality – it is merely a reflection of reality. In his *Republic*, Plato records Socrates as saying we are like people living in a cave, and the sun outside casts shadows. We give names to these shadows, thinking they are reality when the actual reality is outside the cave. True philosophy is grasping that *something* is casting those shadows on the wall, and that *something* is so much more than the shadowland's drab and dull world.

In his *Republic*, Plato explained his ideal society - *not* a democracy. His utopia had philosopher-kings making wise decisions for the *hoi polloi* (common folk) because philosophers could see the actual reality - not just the cave shadows. The next tier was warriors who protected the people and enforced the law. The third tier was the workers and artisans. He forbade art, for it was only a crude representation of reality.

Aristotle - the tutor of Alexander the Great - believed all creation seeks divine perfection. God created everything with purpose and order - which, when discovered, point to his existence. God is perfect; thus, he is unchanging because perfection cannot be perfected - he is the eternal apex of knowledge and being - the unmoved mover.

The "Father of Logic," Aristotle taught deduction: if the premises (commonly held truths about something) were true, the conclusion is correct. For instance, if our first premise is that all whales are mammals, and our second premise is that all mammals are warm-blooded, we can correctly conclude that all whales are warm-blooded. We can change out whales for gerbils, and the premises and conclusion would be the same. But we can't insert fish as being mammals and warm-blooded because those premises wouldn't be true. From deduction, we can move to induction - from specific truths to universal, generalized knowledge.

Other philosophers worth mentioning include the Cynics and Hedonists. The eccentric Diogenes promoted Cynicism - the belief that happiness comes when one aligns with nature, unencumbered by the desire for riches, fame, or power, living in simplicity without possessions. Diogenes wandered around Athens, holding a lantern to men's faces, looking for a genuinely honest man. He lived in a rain barrel and was known for brutal honesty and shameless disregard for social graces, even urinating in public.

Aristippus taught Hedonism - the belief that pleasure or satisfying one's desires is the greatest good; pursuing pleasure is what we're supposed to do. However, he clarified that one should not become a slave to any pleasure or the money needed to buy it - "possessing, but not possessed." Hedonism was not necessarily being self-absorbed or selfish - one can experience pleasure by bringing pleasure to others. Aristippus said we should follow laws - not because they are good, but because breaking them brings unpleasurable punishment.

Rhetoric - persuasion through eloquent figures of speech and other techniques - was refined into an art form in Classical Greece. Rhetoric could be employed in political speeches, philosophical discussions, or juridical arts (persuading a judge or jury). Several outstanding orators and speechwriters were Lysias, Antisthenes, Demosthenes, and Hypereides.

Lysias was a wealthy immigrant in Athens who narrowly escaped from the 30 tyrants after the Peloponnesian War - they were hunting down foreigners and making them drink hemlock. Lysias got away, but the tyrants got his money, so he supported himself by writing speeches for presentation in the law courts. Lysias' orations used simple, everyday vocabulary and humor; they flowed easily, and he artistically adapted each speech to the specific client. They were elegant and subtle, yet vigorous.

Antisthenes studied rhetoric under Gorgias but later became Socrates' student and an ascetic cynic. His writings were more philosophical than for public or judicial speeches. His stylish and well-crafted writing used smooth discourse, wit, ingenuity, and Socrates' question-and-answer method. He felt his most outstanding achievement in learning philosophy was "'The power to hold a conversation with myself."

Demosthenes was an Athenian political leader, lawyer, speechwriter, and orator. He gave his first judicial speech defending himself in court at age 20 when his rhetorical prowess won him back his inheritance. Interestingly for an orator, he had a speech impediment and engaged in intense training to overcome it. His speeches reflected a powerful intellect, articulate use of facts, and confidence in the justice of his cause.

Hypereides was another Athenian orator who joined Demosthenes in resisting Phillip of Macedon. His political speeches stirred up the revolt against Macedonia, for which he was later executed. Hypereides was a hedonistic epicurean who enjoyed gourmet food and beautiful women. His orations were plain, graceful, witty, and subtle.

Three notable historians supplied vital information about the people and affairs of the Classical Age: Herodotus, Thucydides, and Xenophon. Herodotus wrote *The Histories*, offering invaluable details of the Greco-Persian Wars. Not only did he report on noteworthy events and kings, but he also imparted rich knowledge of the cultures, geographic facts, and fascinating legends. Herodotus was born in the Greek city of Halicarnassus (in present-day Turkey) when it was part of the Persian-Achaemenid Empire. He and his family took part in the struggle between the Greeks and Persia.

Thucydides, the first "scientific" historian, wrote *The History of the Peloponnesian War.* A scientific historian writes with neutrality, using meticulous research, analyzing chain events, and omitting references to the gods' intervention. General Thucydides fought against Sparta in the war, got the plague, survived, and went into exile for 20 years after arriving too late to rescue Amphipolis from Spartan control. He spent those 20 years in the Peloponnese, getting to know his former enemies.

Xenophon was born in Athens but fought with the *Ten Thousand* mercenaries for Cyrus the Younger in Cyrus' failed campaign to steal the Persian throne from his brother Artaxerxes II – recorded in *Anabasis.* His *Cyropaedia* records how Cyrus the Great successfully conquered the Neo-Babylonian Empire. Xenophon wrote *Memorabilia* in honor of his teacher Socrates' life, along with several dialogues in which Socrates was the protagonist and an account of Socrates' trial. His *Hellenica* picked up where Thucydides left off on the Peloponnesian War. Xenophon supplied a rare glimpse into Spartan history and culture in the *Constitution of the Lacedaemonians* and *Agesilaus* – his biography of his friend, the Spartan king.

Did you know the Classical Greek scientists and philosophers Leucippus and his student Democritus developed the rudiments of nuclear physics and atomic theory? They proposed that:

> 1. Atoms – separated by and moving through space (void) – form matter.
>
> 2. Atoms are solid, indivisible, unchanging, and have the same or similar structure.
>
> 3. Changes in matter happen when groupings of atoms change.
>
> 4. Atoms have varied sizes and shapes.
>
> 5. Properties of matter depend on the properties of the atoms it holds.

Democritus also contributed to the earliest understanding of genetics by proposing that both the father and mother produce seeds made up of elements from each organ of their bodies – and that the combined seeds grow into the new embryo.

Another innovation of the Classical Age was battle strategy – in particular, the *Loxi Falagga* (oblique phalanx) designed and implemented by Thebe's General Epaminondas. Since the Archaic age, Greece used the phalanx strategy, with men lined up with shields slightly overlapping. As the line approached the enemy, the soldiers would hold their shields in their left hand and try to tuck the right side of their body behind their neighbor's shield. With each man softly pushing the man to his right, the phalanx line usually veered to the right as the two armies approached each other. Thus, a general would usually place his most potent force on the right.

Epaminondas's masterpiece strategy in the Battle of Leuctra involved an ingenious change to the traditional phalanx formation. Instead of a broad line of soldiers 12-ranks deep, he had four sets of phalanxes, beginning with a shorter mega-phalanx on his left side (the side facing the Spartans' stronger right side) that was 50 ranks deep. He put three other phalanx formations – his weaker warriors – in three thinner lines to the right and slightly behind the mega-phalanx. He also put his best warriors – the Sacred Band – in the front row of the mega-phalanx.

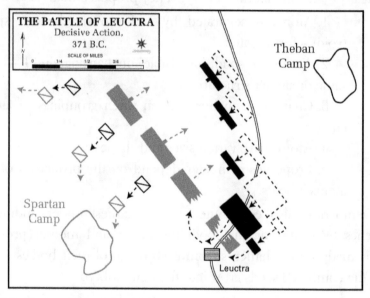

This diagram displays the innovative phalanx strategy used in the Battle of Leuctra.

https://upload.wikimedia.org/wikipedia/commons/7/7a/Battle_of_Leuctra%2C_3 71_BC_-_Decisive_action.png

His plan was for the mega-phalanx to crush the strongest, right side of the Spartan phalanx, then turn and outflank the rest of the Spartan line, engaging with the other three Theban phalanxes – which had added protection from the Theban cavalry. And it worked! The unthinkable happened – the unassailable Spartan right flank crumbled.

The Classical Period was Greece's "coming of age" – maturing in the arts, literature, science, mathematics, and philosophy – all while achieving victory over Persia, then engaging in fierce internecine conflict in the Peloponnesian, Corinthian, and Theban-Spartan wars. More war was to come – the threat of Macedonia loomed on the horizon.

Chapter 11: The Rise of Macedonia and Phillip II

"Oh, how small a portion of earth will hold us when we are dead, who ambitiously seek after the entire world while we are living!"

~ Philip II of Macedon

While the Greek power struggles raged between Athens, Sparta, and Thebes, Macedon was nothing more than an obscure kingdom on the northern periphery of the Greek world. In 359 BCE, when Philip II ascended the throne, Macedonia lay on the verge of ruination. The Athenians had raided and claimed two of their towns, the Illyrians had killed their king, and Macedonia's weak military was hardly a match for their stronger enemies.

But Philip II, the new king, was an ambitious young man who would strikingly reform the military and prepare to launch one of the most staggering expeditions of ancient times. During his reign and his son Alexander's, Macedonia would rise from an insignificant "barbarian" kingdom, rife with inner turmoil, to an astounding empire – albeit a short-lived one.

Macedonia's Argead dynasty descended from the mythical King Temenus of Argos, according to Herodotus and Thucydides. Persia invaded during King Amyntas I's reign (548-498 BCE), making Macedon a vassal of the Achaemenid Empire. Amyntas' son King Alexander I supplied military forces to Xerxes I when he invaded Greece in 480 BCE. Persia's apocalyptic defeat at Salamis in 480 BCE forced its withdrawal from Greece, leaving Macedonia a free city-state.

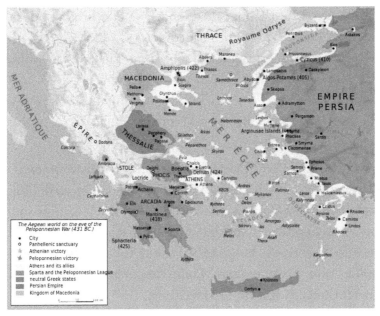

This map depicts Macedonia's location and size at the beginning of the Peloponnesian War – similar to when Philip assumed the throne.

https://commons.wikimedia.org/wiki/File:Map_Peloponnesian_War_431_BC-en.svg

Amyntas' sons Alexander, Perdiccas, and Phillip II were born into this chaos. Alexander developed friendships with both Athens and Sparta, but his successor Perdiccas II fought with Sparta at the beginning of the Peloponnesian War, then switched sides to Athens. Perdiccas' son King Archelaus I developed Macedonia as a spectacular cultural center, attracting the playwright Euripides to his court. Archelaus's page and former lover Craterus assassinated him, usurping the throne for four days until Archelaus' young son Orestes gained control. Orestes ruled for three years until his uncle Aeropus II murdered him and became king, succeeded by his son Pausanias. Amyntas III assassinated his relative Pausanias and took the throne, ruling from 393-370 BCE.

Philip II spent his childhood in the turmoil of family assassinations and his teen years as a hostage in foreign lands. When he was 12, his father died, and his older brother Alexander II became king. But their mother's lover, Ptolemy of Aloros, murdered her son Alexander II and sent Philip as a hostage to Illyria. This attack on the princes caused an uprising in Macedonia. General Pelopidas of Thebes intervened, putting Philip's brother Perdiccas III on the throne and taking Philip as a hostage to Thebes.

In Thebes, General Pelopidas made Philip his *eromenos* (boy sexual partner), and his friend Epaminondas educated Philip in military arts and diplomacy. Thebes was still reveling in its stunning victory over Sparta at Leuctra, which had shaken Greece's power balance to its core. As he absorbed astute military knowledge from Pelopidas and Epaminondas, Philip began to formulate his own designs for military reform in Macedonia.

Philip returned to Macedonia at age 17, schooled in Theban military tactics. When he was 23, the Illyrians killed his brother, King Perdiccas II, abruptly bringing Philip to the throne in 359 BCE. With Illyria and Paeonia threatening invasion, Philip at once went to work reforming his army – implementing the knowledge he had learned as a hostage – in his first step in metamorphosizing his newly-acquired humble kingdom into a soaring new empire.

Most importantly, Philip introduced a lethal new weapon he'd invented – the sarissa! This mega-spear was 13 to 20 feet long and weighed 12 to 14 pounds! Its streamlined iron tip could penetrate armor and the person in it. Macedonian iron or bronze formed a butt at the other end of the sarissa that supplied counterweight, so the warrior could balance it horizontally or plant it in the ground to brace for the charging enemy.

The Macedonian Phalanx -- Philip's brainchild - featured the exceptionally long sarissa.

Drawing by B. F. Mitchell, Department of History, United States Military Academy.

https://commons.wikimedia.org/w/index.php?curid=498246http://www.au.af.mil/au/awc/awcgate/gabrmetz/gabr0066.htm, Public Domain.

The extreme length and weight of the sarissa spear required the soldier to hold it in both hands, which meant he couldn't carry a heavy shield. Philip had his hoplites carry smaller *pelta* shields strapped to their left arms. The extra-long sarissa was deadly in Philip's new Macedonian phalanx - another novel idea. Philip's phalanx had 16 lines of men but was only eight men wide! Instead of just one massive phalanx, he had multiple, smaller phalanxes following bugle messages, flag signals, and a herald who called out orders. These smaller phalanxes were more mobile and could wheel around to face an enemy's attempt to outflank them.

As the phalanx approached the enemy, the soldiers held their sarissas upright until close to their enemy. Then, the phalanx's first five rows dropped their spears into a horizontal position, leaving a formidable line of fatal spearheads facing the enemy. In the lines behind the first five rows, the soldiers held their lances at a 45-

degree angle over the soldiers' heads in front, deflecting enemy arrows. Philip also copied Epaminondas' Sacred Band – forming his own full-time elite corps – *the pezhetairoi*, who fought on the far-right end of the unassailable phalanx.

Not only was Philip a master military strategist, but he cunningly formed allies. Like his ancestor Archelaus I, he strove to develop Pella – his capital city – into a literature and philosophy cultural center. He invited Aristotle to tutor his son Alexander, and he invited rulers from throughout Greece to send their sons to Pella to join Alexander in Aristotle's school, knowing the fathers would not attack Macedonia if their prince were living there!

Queen Olympias, pictured on a gold coin, was Philip's fourth wife, a princess of Epirus, and mother of Alexander the Great.
https://commons.wikimedia.org/wiki/File:Coin_olympias_mus_theski.JPG

Philip was adept at brilliant marriage alliances. Unlike most Greeks, the Macedonian kings could have more than one wife, and Philip had at least seven – princesses of his neighboring city-states. All his wives were queens, and the children of all wives were royal. He formed alliances with Illyria, Elimiotis (Upper Macedonia), Thessaly, Epirus, and Thrace through marriage.

In 358 BCE, only one year into his reign, Philip expanded his kingdom of Macedonia to the north, east, and south. Within 25 years, Macedonia would dominate Greece. He first defeated the Paeonians to the north of Macedonia. His biggest threat was the Illyrians in the northeast, who had killed his brother and were preparing to invade again. Philip reaped his revenge by killing 7000 Illyrians in one battle, pushing his rule as far as present-day Albania.

The following year, Philip laid siege to Athens' colony of Amphipolis, taking control of the gold and silver mines in Mount Pangaion. When Athens protested, he offered them the lease of Amphipolis in exchange for the coastal town of Pydna, which had been Macedonian territory but stolen by Athens. But then Philip conquered Pydna for himself. That same year, he married his fourth wife Olympias, and she gave birth to Alexander in the following year.

In 356 BCE, Philip overcame the city of Crenides, changing its name to Philippi and setting up a garrison there to protect its gold mines. Meanwhile, a second Macedonian force put down another invasion attempt by the Illyrians. In a sequence of brutal campaigns (356-340 BCE) against Thrace to Macedonia's northwest, Philip subdued its King Kersebleptes, making Thrace a tributary city-state.

In addition to his indomitable phalanx, Philip's engineers devised devastating siege engines to bring down defensive walls. His cavalry was also a force to reckon with – one in seven soldiers were equestrians carrying a sword and either a sarissa or a 9-foot javelin. His cavalry, organized into 120 to 300 horse squadrons, would first charge in a wedge-shaped formation with spears in hand. Once they'd impaled an enemy, they'd switch to sword fights.

This bust of Philip II is a Roman copy of a Greek original.

https://commons.wikimedia.org/wiki/File:Philip-ii-of-macedon.jpg

Another Sacred War broke out in 356 BCE when Phocis - the city-state next to where the Oracle of Delphi lived - refused to pay a fine to the Thebes-controlled Amphictyonic League for illegally farming the Sacred Land. The Phocians, with Sparta's and Athens' support, seized Delphi, but they lost their aid when they plundered Apollo's treasury to hire mercenaries. Getting involved in this war allowed Philip to expand to central and southern Greece. In a coalition army with Thessaly (against whom he'd been campaigning but now offered a truce to fight with him), Philip pulverized the Phocians in 352 BCE at the Battle of Crocus Field, killing 6000 and capturing 3000. Philip's constant battles over the years cost him an eye and crippled him in the shoulder and leg.

After the Sacred War, Thessaly made Philip its *archon* (ruler) for life, dramatically increasing his power. After getting things settled in Thessaly, Philip marched toward southern Greece, but an Athenian force held him off at the Thermopylae Pass - the same place where the Spartans held off the Persians. This time no traitor showed him the secret alternative passage, so Philip postponed his southern campaign. Instead, he focused on subduing the Balkan hill people and successfully laying siege to Olynthus and other coastal cities of northwestern Greece.

Meanwhile, Phocis' General Phalaikos had returned from exile, forbidding Athens and Sparta from accessing the Thermopylae Pass (in Phocis territory) - part of a peace settlement he was arranging with Philip. The Athenians had no way to keep Philip out of southern Greece without defending the pass, so they sent envoys to Philip to discuss peace. In the 346 BCE Peace of Philocrates, Athens agreed to ally with Philip and give up Amphipolis. Philip set up a garrison at the Thermopylae Pass, then headed home to Macedonia. It would be seven years before he returned to southern Greece. He was already conceiving plans for war with Persia, and for that, he would need Athens' navy.

The great Athenian orator Isocrates wrote to Philip in 346 BCE - the year Athens pledged peace with Macedonia. Isocrates urged Philip to reconcile Athens with Sparta, Thebes, and Argos - bringing all the Greeks into unison. Isocrates said that if Philip could unite these four principal cities, the smaller towns would follow suit. He said that instead of each Greek city-state fighting the other Greeks, they needed to fight Persia - together.

"Be assured that a glory unsurpassable and worthy of the deeds you have done in the past will be yours when you shall compel the barbarians—all but those who have fought on your side—to be serfs of the Greeks, and when you shall force the king who is now called Great to do whatever you command."

Isocrates, over 90 years old, died soon after sending the letter to Philip. He knew Philip was already planning war against Persia, and his best chance of success was with a united Greece.

With a massive kingdom, the largest and most lethal army in Greece, and abundant natural resources, Philip dominated Greece. But not everyone was happy with that. The Athenian political leader Demosthenes had always gone on long tirades against Philip, calling him a brat, and now he was even more vicious. He watched Philip like a hawk, constantly accusing him of breaking the terms of peace.

In 340 BCE, Demosthenes convinced the assembly to ally with the Persians in Byzantium – when Philip was besieging them! By joining with Philip's enemy, they declared war against Philip. In 339 BCE, Philip marched to southern Greece. Athens and Thebes quickly allied and welcomed alliances with any other southern Greek states opposed to Philip. Thebes seized the town of Nicaea, blocking Philip's access to the Thermopylae Pass. But this time, Philip knew of another way over the mountains.

In 338 BCE, Philip marched to Boeotia with 30,000 foot-soldiers and 2000 cavalrymen to confront the coalition army of Thebes and Athens in the Battle of Chaeronea. He put his 18-year-old son Alexander in charge of the left-wing phalanx with experienced officers, and he took the lead of the right-wing with his specialized pezhetairoi forces. The Athenians panicked when they learned he'd slipped over the mountains and was only a three-day march away.

The coalition forces spread out in a line extending two-and-a-half miles on the main road leading to Chaeronea. Athens took the left-wing phalanx, facing Philip, Thebes took the right wing, facing Alexander, and Corinth and the other allies were in the middle. Athens' left wing moved forward first, while Thebes' right-wing forces were on the side of a mountain – difficult for Philip to attack uphill.

Philip pulled an old Spartan battle strategy: he cunningly engaged Athens' army briefly, then turned in a fake retreat, with the Athenians charging heavily after. Philip's men dashed as far as a nearby hill, where they abruptly swirled around to attack. They had lured the Athenians off their hill to the other hill – now the Macedonians had the high ground! Meanwhile, Alexander proved himself extraordinarily well against the Thebans – punching a hole in their lines – the first to shatter the ranks of Thebes' legendary Sacred Band!

The epic battle – one of the most decisive in ancient Greece – was over. Macedonia had won! Corinth and Athens rushed home to fortify their defensive walls, expecting Philip to show up with his siege engines any moment. But he didn't. Philip didn't want to destroy their cities – he wanted them to join him against Persia. He especially wanted Athens' navy!

Philip also had to deal with Sparta, who had not gotten involved against Macedonia. He didn't want Sparta to attack nearby cities when their warriors were overseas with him. When he invited the Spartans to negotiations, they tersely refused to talk, so Philip razed the region of Lacedaemonia around Sparta but left the city alone.

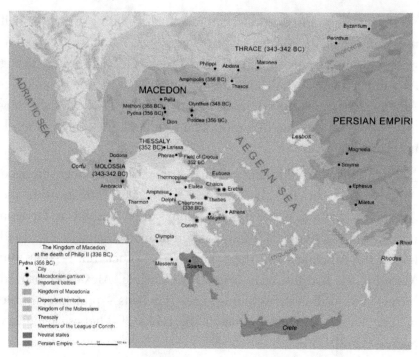

This map depicts Macedonia's expanded borders and alliances with all Greece except Sparta as Philip prepared to launch a war against the Persian Empire.

https://commons.wikimedia.org/wiki/File:Map_Macedonia_336_BC-en.svg

Philip installed garrisons throughout central and southern Greece. While encamped near Corinth, he formed a council to negotiate a new league of city-states to ensure peace in Greece and provide the men and supplies for Philip's planned war on Persia. The Greek city-states united under the League of Corinth, set up in 337 BCE to lead a coordinated revolt against the Persian Empire. It included all the city-states – except Sparta. All members of the league solemnly pledged not to attack a sister city-state or interfere with their internal affairs. The league's leadership then declared war on the Persian-Achaemenid Empire with Philip as their *Strategos* (armed forces commander).

Philip had everything set up to lead a colossal Greek coalition against Persia. He had already sent an advance force of 10,000 men to Asia Minor in preparation for freeing the Greek city-states from Persia. What could stop him now? Murder! He was stabbed to death by his former lover.

Philip's handsome bodyguard Pausanias grew jealous when Philip switched his affections to another young man – also named Pausanias. The first Pausanias publicly reviled the second Pausanias' sexuality and moral character. The second Pausanias did nothing at first but finally told his friend General Attalus (Philip's seventh wife's uncle) that he could no longer bear to live. Several days later, he threw himself in front of Philip in a battle – dying from a hail of arrows aimed at the king.

Attalus avenged his friend by inviting the first Pausanias to a banquet, getting him thoroughly drunk, then raping him. When he sobered up, Pausanias reported the sexual assault to Philip. Although furious, Philip did nothing to punish Attalus, his relative by marriage – he needed Attalus to lead his forces against Persia. He tried to assuage Pausanias with gifts and promotion, but Pausanias' resentment festered – not only against Attalus but now against Philip for not punishing his rapist.

In 336 BCE, in an elaborate royal wedding, Philip gave his daughter Cleopatra (Alexander the Great's sister and daughter of his fourth wife Olympias) to wed Alexander of Epirus. At the festivities, Pausanias suddenly pulled out a dagger and stabbed Philip. He fled but caught his foot on a vine and fell, and Philip's bodyguards ran him through. Macedonia's great warrior-king was dead. Would his legacy continue?

Chapter 12: Alexander the Great

"Through every generation of humanity, a constant war has raged, a war with fear.

Those who have the courage to conquer it are set free,

and those it conquers suffer until they dare to defeat it, or death takes them."

~ Alexander the Great

Was Alexander's mother involved in Philip's murder? Justin and Plutarch characterized Queen Olympias as evil, ruthless, jealous, and vengeful, saying she erected a memorial to Pausanias - her husband's killer, shortly after the murder. Olympias' chief ambition was for Alexander to become the next king. Aside from Alexander, Philip only had one other son -Arrhidaeus - who suffered from epilepsy and intellectual disability.

But everything changed when Philip married his seventh wife - General Attalus' niece Cleopatra Eurydice - with whom Philip had fallen in love. Olympias worried that Cleopatra's children might take precedence over Alexander - as they would be full-blooded Macedonians. A drunken Attalus prayed the marriage would produce a legitimate heir to Philip's throne at the wedding banquet.

At this, Alexander jumped up, shouting, "Are you calling me a bastard?"

His enraged father leaped up to strike him but drunkenly fell. Alexander jeered at Philip, "Look at this! He wants to cross over from Europe into Asia but falls moving from one chair the next!"

Fearing the ramifications of his rash words, Alexander hurried out of town with his mother. But once sober, Philip knew his best successor was Alexander – well trained in all areas and an astute general. Within six months, Alexander returned to his father's court. Cleopatra soon gave birth to a girl named Europa, followed by a boy named Caranus.

Within minutes of Philip's murder, the nobles and military proclaimed 20-year-old Alexander as their new king. Alexander killed his infant half-brother Caranus, and Olympias killed the little girl Europa out of hatred for Cleopatra, who committed suicide. Alexander also ordered the death of General Attalus but spared his disabled brother Arrhidaeus.

Following Philip's death, Athens, Thebes, Thessaly, and Thrace revolted from the League of Corinth. Alexander quickly marched south with 3000 men. The Thessalian army waited for him at the pass between Mount Ossa and Mount Olympus, but Alexander circled over Mount Ossa by night. The Thessalians awoke to find the Macedonians at their rear! The startled Thebans surrendered, and Alexander continued marching south.

At Thermopylae, the Amphictyonic League bowed to him as their leader. Athens apologized for revolting, and Alexander forgave the city – he needed their navy! Corinth gave Alexander the title of *Hegemon* (dominant).

Sebastiano Ricci's painting depicts the encounter between Alexander and Diogenes. https://commons.wikimedia.org/wiki/File:Ricci_-_Diogene_e_Alessandro_Magno,_1680-1695.jpg

Alexander met the Cynic Diogenes in Corinth, sitting in front of his rain barrel, enjoying a sunbath. "What can I do for you?" Alexander asked.

"Move over!" the undiplomatic Diogenes answered. "You're in my light!"

Alexander laughed, "If I weren't Alexander, I would like to be Diogenes!"

With southern Greece back in line, Alexander needed to rein in the openly revolting northern states. In 335 BCE, he soundly defeated the Thracians on Mount Haemus, thrashed Triballi's army, and marched to the Danube. Alexander caught the Getae tribe unaware by crossing the river at night, sending them into retreat. He next marched west, dispatching King Cleitus of Illyria and King Glaukias of the Taulantii, brilliantly securing northern Greece.

But while he was in the north, Athens and Thebes revolted again. Exasperated, Alexander marched south. He razed Thebes, selling the Thebans into slavery, and gave its territory to the Boeotian cities. Hearing of this, Athens immediately submitted.

Alexander was ready to lead a coalition campaign against the Persian Empire superpower with a unified Greece – one of history's most stunning military expeditions of all time. In his astounding 10-year Asian invasion, he established one of the world's greatest empires. Persia called him Alexander the Accursed, but the Greeks soon called him Alexander the Great.

In 334 BCE, Alexander and his skilled General Parmenion crossed into Asia Minor with their 40,000-man coalition forces. General Memnon of Rhodes, a Greek mercenary, warned the Persian generals, "Withdraw to the interior," he advised. "Strip and burn the fields – if he can't feed his army, he'll leave." But the Persian satraps were too proud just to retreat – they would confront Alexander at the River Granicus.

The Battle of Granicus began with the Persians lined up along the steep banks of a shallow river – the Greek forces would have to forge the river and confront the Persians going uphill. Alexander placed his phalanx in the middle of his line, his Thessalian-Thracian cavalry on the left, and he led the right wing with his Macedonian cavalry, his elite pezhetairoi forces, his Bulgarian javelin-throwers, and his expert archers.

The evening was fast approaching, and the Persians expected the Greeks to cross the river at dawn. Instead, Philips unexpectedly attacked immediately and swiftly. Alexander and his right wing forged the river with a cavalry charge, under a hail of arrows and spears, then up the steep bank toward the Persians, who tried to force them back into the river. Alexander plunged his javelin into the face of Mithridates, son-in-law of Darius III. Suddenly, a Persian cavalryman struck Alexander in the head with his scimitar – slicing his helmet in two, but without acute injury to Alexander, who impaled him with his javelin. Another cavalryman raised his sword to strike Alexander from behind. Just in time, Alexander's friend Black Cleitus sliced off the Persian's arm.

Alexander was 22 when he left Greece on his enthralling campaign against Persia. https://commons.wikimedia.org/wiki/File:Alexander_the_Great-Ny_Carlsberg_Glyptotek.jpg

By then, the rest of the army had crossed, forming an invincible wall of 18-foot sarissas. The Persians had never encountered a phalanx with spears three times their body length! In a frenzy, they spun around, in full retreat! Alexander scored an epic victory, breaking Persian power over the Greek city-states of Asia-Minor.

As Alexander marched toward Sardis - the capital of Lydia, its satrap surrendered at once. Before marching further, Alexander had to shut down Persia's deadly armada. Rather than fighting the ships, Alexander attacked their bases - Miletus and Halicarnassus. With non-functional bases, Persia's naval fleet was no longer a significant threat.

In 333 BCE, Alexander advanced into Lycia and Phrygia. At Phrygia's capital of Gordium, Alexander encountered the "Gordian Knot." According to an oracle, any man who could untie it would rule Asia. Alexander glanced at the entangled mass, then drew his sword and sliced it in two. He'd undone the knot - Asia was his for the taking!

Alexander was marching into Cilicia when King Darius's mammoth army approached from the rear, trapping Alexander between the Nur mountains and Darius' army spread across Issus' coastal plain. Alexander quickly formed his army into the same positions as at Granicus: Parmenion leading the Greek allies on the left, the Macedonian phalanx in the center, and Alexander on the right with his elite infantry and cavalry.

As at Granicus, Darius lined up along the Pinarus River. Alexander attacked full-speed - his horsemen galloping across the river, but the foot soldiers had trouble crossing the river on foot, with their armor and long spears. Alexander charged his Macedonian cavalry straight into the Persian infantry at the center, throwing them into an uproar, while the Macedonian infantry regrouped into proper phalanx position.

Darius III of Persia in the Alexander Mosaic from Pompeii,
depicting his battle against Alexander the Great. The Mosaic is
believed to be a copy of a third-century BCE painting.
https://en.wikipedia.org/wiki/Darius_III#/media/File:Darius_III_mosaic.jpg

As Alexander charged toward King Darius, he paled at the sight of the insanely intrepid Macedonian. Whirling his chariot around, Darius raced off. Meanwhile, Parmenion's left wing was desperately fending off the elite Persian cavalry. Would they outflank the Greeks? Not on the dogged Parmenion's watch! His men held off the Persians until word swept through their forces that Darius had abandoned the field.

Bewildered, the Persians stood still for a moment – were they supposed to stay and fight? Or follow their king? One look at the Macedonians' bristling sarissas settled the question. Run! The Greeks chased after, slaughtering them left and right. Although a sword sliced his thigh, Alexander won a brilliant victory at the Battle of Issus and captured Darius' mother, wife, and two daughters, whom he cared for with respect, later marrying one of the daughters – Stateira II.

In 332 BCE, all the coastal cities of Phoenicia but one surrendered to Alexander, ending Persia's naval power in the Mediterranean. The one hold-out was Tyre – the ancient city in Lebanon that had ruled the waves for 2000 years. Its warriors fought fiercely – attacking the causeway Alexander built over to the island and his siege towers with their fire ships, but the city fell after seven months.

Between Phoenicia and Egypt lay Gaza. Alexander's engineers told him the city's high hill made it impossible for their siege engines to break the formidable walls. Nothing was impossible for Alexander. His engineers built hills to bring their siege engines high enough to launch missiles at Gaza. While they were doing this, the men of Gaza came out of the city to attack the siege engines, and an arrow pierced Alexander's shield, lodging in his shoulder, seriously wounding him. After three failed attempts, the walls of Gaza fell.

Egypt put up no resistance. Egypt's Persian satrap handed the province and its treasury to Alexander. The priests at Memphis crowned him as Pharaoh, exulting that Alexander had rescued them from Persian rule. Alexander founded the city of Alexandria at the mouth of the Nile, which quickly developed into a breathtaking Hellenistic center. At the Siwi Oasis, the Oracle of Amun-Ra pronounced Alexander as the son of Amun – the king of their gods – analogous to the Greek god Zeus. After this, Alexander spoke of Zeus – or Amun – as his father, expecting everyone to recognize his divinity.

In 331 BCE, as Alexander's father Philip had feared, Sparta took advantage of Alexander and his Greek allies being overseas and launched a war against the coalition cities. General Antipater, Alexander's regent in Greece, marched to the Peloponnese to confront Sparta's King Agis III. The legendary Spartan war machine was no match for the Macedonian phalanx: King Agis and 5300 Spartan warriors died in the Battle of Megalopolis.

With Sparta permanently subdued, Alexander was ready to conquer the rest of Persia's Empire. King Darius wrote him, offering his daughter in marriage, half his empire, and a gold fortune if Alexander would go home. Alexander laughed. He already had both daughters, and he wanted all Persia – not half! He met Darius in battle at Gaugamela in Iraq. Darius had about twice as many men as Alexander – with chariots and war elephants – a new challenge for the Greeks!

Alexander charged his cavalry around the Persian's left flank. Darius moved his center troops to block Alexander from encircling him, but Alexander's cavalry then charged through the thinned middle line. Darius sent his chariots out, but the Bulgarian javelin-throwers decimated the horses and men. Once again, Darius fled the battle as Scythian and Indian cavalry encircled Parmenion's left-wing force. Alexander raced to aid Parmenion in bloody combat that killed 60 of his elite cavalry. But once the Persians realized their king had retreated, they likewise fled. Now Alexander marched unhindered to Babylon, the principal capital of the Persian-Achaemenid Empire, acclaimed by the people as the ruler of Persia.

Alexander chased Darius to Media, but the former king slipped away east, with Alexander close behind. Before Alexander could reach him, Darius's Bactrian governor Bessus murdered Darius – the last Persian-Achaemenid king – proclaiming himself king. Alexander ordered a royal burial for his rival, then turned his attention to organizing his new empire. He appointed viceroys to govern his provinces, keeping any Persian governors who swore allegiance to him.

Alexander's next goal was to hunt down the assassin Bessus – and kill him – on his way to the "edge of the world," conquering the eastern provinces on the way. In Afghanistan, he put down a revolt by Governor Satibarzanes, who had sworn fake allegiance to Alexander. With Satibarzanes dead, he pursued Bessus, whose Bactrian chieftains betrayed him, chaining him to a stake for Alexander to find. Alexander sent him to Persia for execution.

Despite his stunning victories, Alexander's army was weary of war. Alexander learned that Philotas – commander of his cavalry and General Parmenion's son – knew of an assassination plot against Alexander but had done nothing. Alexander executed him and sent assassins to kill Parmenion. He could no longer trust his distinguished general and friend.

Alexander pressed east, founding Alexandria-*Eschate* (the *furthest*) on the Jaxartes River. He had reached the far eastern boundary of the Persian-Achaemenid Empire. Although an arrow broke his fibula (calf bone), he crushed an attack of the nomadic Scythians but was frustratingly unable to subdue the guerilla attacks of the Bactrians and Sogdians. A stone struck Alexander's head at the 329 BCE Siege of Cyropolis, rendering him temporarily blind and unable to speak.

Alexander's troops were increasingly restive and dispirited. They longed to see home again, but Alexander was unstoppable – and irritating – dressing in Persian clothing and expecting people to drop to the floor before him in reverence. His mercurial moods became deadly when he murdered his close friend in a drunken brawl – Cleitus the Black – who had saved his life. Once sober, Alexander was grief-stricken and remorseful, but his growing arrogance and erratic behavior alienated him from his military. Another assassination plot came to light in Bactria. Hermolaus, a royal page, and his accomplices were stoned to death.

In the summer of 327 BCE, Alexander captured and fell in love with Roxana, the beautiful daughter of the Sogdian Lord Oxyartes of Bactria, who surrendered after Alexander seized his family. Despite the objections of his generals, he married Roxana, then appointed his father-in-law as governor of the Hindu Kush

Mountain region in hopes Oxyartes would bring the rest of the Sogdians and Bactrians in line.

Alexander crossed the towering, snow-covered Hindu Kush mountains at the 3500-foot Khyber Pass, fighting the fierce Aspasii and Assaceni tribes and descending into the Indian subcontinent. He faced off against King Porus of Pauravas on opposite banks of the monsoon-swollen Hydaspes (Jhelum) River, whose churning waters made crossing impossible. Alexander kept most of his forces out of sight, so Porus would think the Greek army was smaller. His cavalry rode up and down the river by night, finally finding a shallow spot to cross 17 miles upstream.

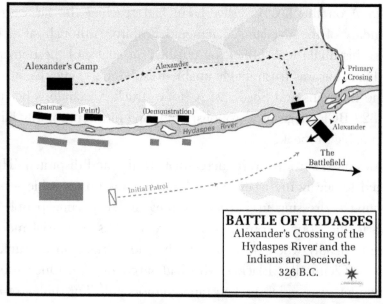

Alexander's battle tactics enabled him to defeat King Porus and his formidable war elephants. By Frank Martini. Cartographer, Department of History, United States Military Academy - The Department of History, United States Military Academy [1], Public Domain, https://commons.wikimedia.org/w/index.php?curid=34909073

General Craterus remained behind with part of Alexander's forces, engaging in antics at the riverside to distract Porus from realizing the rest of the army was on the move. Silently and out of sight, Alexander's troops traipsed upstream, crossing the river with the foot-soldiers holding to skin floats or in small boats. Once they crossed, Alexander and his men, as quietly as possible, moved down the opposite bank to meet the Indian forces, who finally realized they were coming and quickly assembled into ranks.

Alexander used a *pincer maneuver* against Porus, flanking both sides of his army with his cavalry. The Indian war elephants advanced but met a wall of bristling sarissas. Although the elephants killed many Greeks at the Battle of the Hydaspes, the sarissas eventually routed the panicked animals, who ran back, crushing as many Indians as they had Greeks. Using *a hammer and anvil maneuver* – with one small force attacking or holding ground, while a second quickly encircled the enemy – the Greeks put the entire Indian army on the run. Alexander's decisive victory brought him control of the Punjab region.

THE WAR ELEPHANT OF INDIA.

The Greek soldiers fought Indian war elephants in the Battle of the Hydaspes.

https://commons.wikimedia.org/wiki/File:The_war_elephant_of_Inida..jpg

Alexander was eager to continue to the great river of India – the "edge of the world." But his men mutinied. They'd been away from their families for years. They'd heard massive armies were preparing to meet them in India. An incensed Alexander had no choice but to follow the Indus River on a 10-month journey south to the Arabian Sea. Half the army sailed back to Persia through the Persian Gulf – exploring waters the Greek fleets had never sailed. Alexander and the rest trekked through the Gedrosian (Makran) desert, one-third of his men dying from extreme heat and lack of water. Reaching Persia, a grateful Alexander paid off his soldiers' debts.

Then it was time for a wedding! Alexander threw an enormous feast celebrating the collective marriage of 80 Persian princesses to Macedonian officers - uniting Greece and Persia through intermarrying the leading families. Alexander married two ladies in one day: Princesses Stateira II - daughter of King Darius III and Parysatis II - daughter of Artaxerxes III. Alexander soon received the joyous news that his beloved first wife, Roxanna, was pregnant. But he would never hold his only child in his arms.

While planning a campaign to Arabia in 323 BCE, a fever struck Alexander - within two weeks, the invincible warrior, who survived countless battles, was gone. Only 32, Alexander died, having never lost a battle. His brilliant and fearless military exploits continue to amaze and inspire. He conquered one country after another to create a rule stretching from the Indus Valley to Greece - one of the world's greatest empires.

Alexander was placed in a gold sarcophagus filled with honey. On its way to Macedon for burial, Ptolemy - Alexander's general who made himself Pharaoh of Egypt, founding the Ptolemaic Dynasty - stole the coffin. Alexander's casket remained in Alexandria, Egypt, for centuries, visited by Rome's emperors.

Alexander gave his name to new cities he founded throughout his campaign - naming 70 cities Alexandria - and naming one new settlement after his horse! Alexandria of Egypt is the most eminent, the largest city on the Mediterranean today. After the Battle at the Hydaspes, Alexander named the city he founded Bucephala - after his famous black stallion Bucephalus who died in the battle.

Alexander and Bucephalus as depicted in the Battle of Issus Mosaic.

https://commons.wikimedia.org/wiki/File:Alexander_and_Bucephalus_-_Battle_of_Issus_mosaic_-_Museo_Archeologico_Nazionale_-_Naples_BW.jpg

Alexander's astounding battle strategies are still studied at West Point and other military academies today. Carthage's Hannibal Barca implemented the pincer maneuver Alexander used against Porus to surround and destroy a vast Roman army at the Battle of Cannae. The USA used this strategy against Iraqi tanks in the first Gulf War.

"When my casket is carried to the grave, leave my hands hanging outside.

For empty-handed, I came into this world, and empty-handed, I shall go!

My whole life has been a hallow waste, a futile exercise,

for no one at death can take anything with them!"

~Alexander the Great

PART THREE: THE HELLENISTIC PERIOD (323-31 BCE)

Chapter 13: Diadochi: The Partition of an Empire

"It is a fact that we tribes of suffering men never plant our feet firmly upon the path of joy,

but there is ever some bitter pain to keep company with our delight."

~Apollonius of Rhodes, *Jason and the Golden Fleece*

Alexander's sudden death with no plans for a successor left the empire in chaos. In only ten years, Alexander the Great had carved out an astonishing empire; yet it was unstable and quickly crumbled after his death. His generals vied for power, dividing the empire into three dominant kingdoms from the vast empire Alexander left behind – each forging a new dynasty that persisted for several hundred years. The Antigonus dynasty ruled Macedon, the Ptolemy family reigned as the new pharaohs of Egypt, and the Seleucus dynasty ruled the vast Seleucid-Persian Empire.

Alexander the Great's death marked the beginning of the intriguing Hellenistic Period when the Greek world transformed from autonomous city-states to several large kingdoms. In the ten incredible years Alexander and his troops spent in Asia and Egypt, they assimilated aspects of the foreign cultures while leaving their own cultural footprints. *Koine* (common dialect) Greek was now the western Mediterranean's *lingua franca* (shared language*)*.

The Wars of the *Diadochi* (successors) raged for decades between Alexander's family, generals, and friends – bitter rivals over the empire's control. When Alexander died, he had four closely-related family members: his half-brother Arrhidaeus (Philip III), who struggled with cognitive issues, his mother Olympias, his half-sister Eurydice, and his full sister Cleopatra. Alexander's wife Roxana was pregnant when he died, giving birth three months later to a son, Alexander IV.

This mosaic from Pella, Macedonia, shows Alexander (on the left) with Craterus in a lion hunt.
https://commons.wikimedia.org/w/index.php?curid=1470489

Craterus was a general who had commanded both Alexander's infantry and navy. In 324 BCE, Alexander sent Craterus home to be his regent in Macedonia and called Antipater, his current regent, to join him in Persia as commander of fresh troops. But Alexander died before they made the switch.

On his death bed, Alexander gave his ring to General Perdiccas, signifying Perdiccas was his successor – or regent for his half-brother Arrhidaeus and Roxana's unborn child. When Perdiccas met with the other generals to discuss what to do about the empire, he suggested they wait until Roxana – due in three months – gave birth.

If the baby were a boy, he would be the next king – with Perdiccas as regent and de facto ruler until the boy came of age.

Although the generals had misgivings, the majority agreed to the plan. But General Ptolemy pointed out that Roxana was a conquered captive –her child would be the conquered ruling the conquerors. Agreeing with Ptolemy, General Meleager proposed Arrhidaeus be the next king – King Philip's son and Alexander's half-brother. The soldiers who had crashed the meeting roared their approval, drowning out anyone trying to point out that Arrhidaeus lacked the intellect to rule.

No one had thought to ask Arrhidaeus. Meleager brought him into the room, but in the ensuing uproar, Arrhidaeus scampered away, trembling in fear. Someone coaxed him back in, and they wrapped him in his brother's royal robe. Meleager had the soldiers in such a state that Perdiccas fled to the Euphrates River, fearful for his life. The next day, Arrhidaeus reported Meleager had been bullying him into arresting Perdiccas. It was evident to everyone Meleager was manipulating the vulnerable young man.

Weeping, Arrhidaeus held up the crown, saying anyone qualified to take it should have it. Finally, the assembly decided they would have *two* kings – Arrhidaeus and Roxana's child – and a triumvirate of chiefs: Arrhidaeus, Perdiccas, and Meleager. However, the next day, Perdiccas' men complained vehemently about Meleager being co-chief, and his elite infantry murdered Meleager.

Finally, the leading generals produced a plan – the *Partition of Babylon*. Arrhidaeus and Roxana's child (assuming it was a son) would be joint kings. Perdiccas would be regent and supreme commander of the empire's army. Under Perdiccas' guidance, Arrhidaeus married his niece Eurydice, the daughter of his half-sister Cynane. The empire would remain in the current satrapies (states or territories) stretching from Greece to India. No boundaries would change until 300 BCE.

In the Babylon Partition, the Macedonian General Ptolemy got Egypt. He founded the Ptolemaic Dynasty that lasted three centuries – Egypt's last dynasty.

By Stella - This file has been extracted from another file: British Museum Egypt - Tolomeo I.png, CC BY-SA 4.0, https://commons.wikimedia.org/w/index.php?curid=78788394

What about the rest of Alexander's empire? Greece's mainland – including Macedon and Illyria – went to Antipater, Alexander's regent for the past ten years. Craterus would share Greece's rule. Caria (in today's western Turkey) went to Antipater's son Cassander. General Ptolemy got Egypt, Libya, and Arabia. Antigonus the One-Eyed got Greater Phrygia, Lycia, and Pamphylia. Laomedon got Syria, and Arcesilaus got Mesopotamia. Asian leaders already in place led most of the other provinces.

Athens inflamed other Greek cities into joining the Lamian War of 322 BCE: a belligerent revolt against Antipater. Joining forces with Antipater, Craterus defeated the Athenian force in Thessaly. The Greek cities sued for peace, ending resistance to Macedonian rule; Antipater placed a garrison in Athens and replaced their democracy with an oligarchy.

Two months after the Babylon Partition, Roxana gave birth to a son – Alexander IV. Savagely, Perdiccas colluded with Roxana to kill Alexander's other two wives: Stateira and Parysatis. Then, Perdiccas' men rebelled and killed him, forcing the leading generals and Queen Eurydice to adjust the original Babylon Partition to the 131 BCE *Partition of Triparadisus,* which ended the First War of the Diadochi.

In the new agreement, Antipater replaced Perdiccas as regent over Alexander IV and the cognitively deficient Arrhidaeus, with Arrhidaeus' wife Eurydice as a de facto regent. Antipater moved King Alexander IV, King Philip III (Arrhidaeus), Queen Eurydice, and Roxana to his court in Macedon, continuing his reign over all Greece. Antipater's son Cassander served as the military commander. General Seleucus now ruled Babylon.

The generals continued to squabble over various parts of the empire for the next 40 years. Antipater had been holding the empire together but died just two years later – announcing Polyperchon – another of Alexander's generals – as the succeeding regent. Enraged at being passed over, Antipater's son Cassander drove Polyperchon out of Macedon with the support of Ptolemy and One-Eyed Antigonus, setting Arrhidaeus (Philip III) up as sole king.

Polyperchon fled with little King Alexander IV and Roxana to Epirus, where he allied with Alexander the Great's mother Olympias, who had returned to her homeland. In 317 BCE, Polyperchon and Olympias led forces to attack Cassander in Macedonia. Queen Eurydice and King Philip Arrhidaeus marched out to meet them, but their army defected to Olympias and Polyperchon, refusing to fight against Alexander the Great's mother. Olympias had Arrhidaeus executed and forced Eurydice to commit suicide.

Meanwhile, Cassander had been rallying the support of Antigonus, Ptolemy, and Lysimachus (another of Alexander's generals). He demolished Polyperchon's fleet and overcame Olympias' forces in Pydna. When he ordered his soldiers to execute Olympias, they refused, but the families who had suffered under her stoned her to death. Cassander now had control of Roxana and the boy king Alexander IV.

Polyperchon survived the conflict and now allied with Eumenes, Alexander the Great's personal secretary and commander. Eumenes recruited mercenaries along with 6000 of Alexander's veterans. In 317 BCE, he organized a naval fleet, but Antigonus' fleet destroyed it. After Eumenes and Antigonus fought two vicious but inconclusive land battles in Asia, Antigonus bribed the Argyraspides (Alexander's elite veterans) to hand Eumenes over.

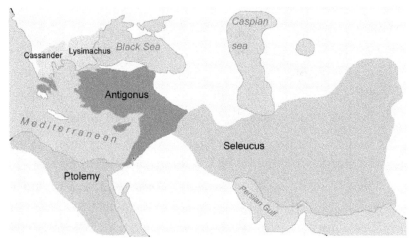

This map depicts territory distribution following the Second War of the Diadochi. https://commons.wikimedia.org/wiki/File:Diadochi.png

After executing Eumenes, Antigonus and Cassander were the victors of the Second War of the Diadochi. Polyperchon had fled to the Peloponnese. Antigonus reigned over the eastern provinces and Asia Minor, Cassander ruled Macedon and substantial portions of Greece, Lysimachus administered Thrace, and Ptolemy kept control of Egypt, Cyprus, Cyrene, and Syria. After a falling out with Antigonus and a brief escape to Egypt, Seleucus would quickly regain control of Babylonia. The powerful generals had few contenders to challenge them.

The eastern Greeks felt Antigonus had too much control over Asia. But they had contenders within – at least Antigonus did. They demanded he hand some of his territories over to Cassander, Lysimachus, Ptolemy, and Seleucus – and he needed to share the booty! Antigonus' response was, "Be ready for war!"

Antigonus invaded Phoenicia and Syria in 314 BCE. Now allied with Polyperchon, he hired Peloponnese mercenaries to fight Cassander. While Antigonus was fighting in Asia Minor, Ptolemy and Seleucus attacked his son Demetrius in the Middle East, defeating him in the Battle of Gaza. Seleucus took back Babylon – his former province. Antigonus returned to Syria to chase Ptolemy back to Egypt and sent Demetrius to deal with Seleucus. Even with his 43 war elephants, Demetrius could not prevail. Antigonus made peace with Cassander, Lysimachus, and Ptolemy, but his attempts to retake the eastern provinces from Seleucus proved unsuccessful.

Meanwhile, people were asking if young Alexander IV still needed a regent. Couldn't he be king on his own when he turned 14 in a few months? Cassander secretly poisoned the boy and his mother Roxana, yet he didn't announce their deaths – the other generals assumed he was still their king. Five Diadochi remained: Cassander over Macedon and Thessaly, Lysimachus reigning over Thrace, Antigonus administering Asia Minor, Phoenicia, and Syria; Seleucus controlling the eastern provinces; and Ptolemy as Pharoah over Egypt and Cyprus.

By 304 BCE, the Wars of the Diadochi were climaxing, with the Battle of Ipsus as the defining contest. Cassander was wrapping up a two-year war with Athens with the victory in sight – until he heard Demetrius had just landed in Boeotia. Cassander called off the siege and quickly marched north to Macedonia, unwilling to be trapped between Demetrius and the Athenians. But he didn't make it – Demetrius intercepted him at Mount Kallidromo, and after 6000 of his Macedonian troops deserted, Cassander scurried away with his remaining troops.

Instead of chasing Cassander, Demetrius headed to the Peloponnese, where he overcame the garrisons at the cities held by Cassander and Ptolemy, declaring the citizens independent. The people of southern Greece (except Sparta, of course) allied under him, proclaiming him "Commander of the Greeks" – as they had Philip II and Alexander the Great. Now Demetrius was ready to confront Cassander – who had been carefully tracking his actions.

But Demetrius was quickly outwearing his welcome in Greece because of his disgraceful predilection for young boys. He pursued a beautiful boy named Democles, desiring him for his eromenos (boy-lover), but the child wanted nothing to do with him. One day he cornered the boy in the baths, and unable to fend him off, Democles jumped in the hot water vat, killing himself.

Meanwhile, Cassander sent envoys to Lysimachus in neighboring Thrace, who agreed to ally with him against Demetrius and Antiochus in Asia Minor. They sent word to Seleucus, who was just returning from fighting in India, bringing with him 500 war elephants! He agreed to join forces with Cassander and Lysimachus and began trekking north to Asia Minor.

This bronze sculpture is of Seleucus, the last Diadochi.
https://commons.wikimedia.org/wiki/File:Seleuco_I_Nicatore.JPG

Expecting an attack from Demetrius, Cassander remained in Macedonia, while Lysimachus instigated a surprise assault in western Asia Minor. Meanwhile, Ptolemy was laying siege to Sidon, Antigonus' city in Syria. The 80-year-old Antigonus swiftly organized his army but discovered another force was arriving from the south – Seleucus' massive troops – elephants and all! Receiving fake news that Antigonus had pulverized the joint forces of Seleucus and Lysimachus, Ptolemy withdrew to Egypt.

Antigonus messaged his son Demetrius to rescue him from the enormous coalition forces. Demetrius crossed over from Greece, meeting up with Antigonus near Ipsus in Phrygia. Their joint forces included 70,000 men and 75 war elephants. Seleucus and Lysimachus had 64,000 infantry in the center and 15,000 cavalry – forming the two flanks. Seleucus lined 200 of his elephants in front of the infantry and kept the rest back.

The showdown began with an elephant charge from both sides, while Demetrius' son Antiochus led a cavalry charge. The outmatched cavalry wheeled and galloped off the field. The center phalanxes had crashed against each other, with Antigonus' more robust line pushing the others back. It was time for Seleucus' secret weapon – the other 300 elephants he'd held back! The beasts successfully blocked Demetrius' cavalry, which had regrouped and was trying to rejoin the battle.

Seleucus' cavalry circled to Antigonus' phalanx's right wing, sending a hail of arrows into their unarmed side. Even as his army disintegrated, the ancient Antigonus fought on, waiting for Demetrius to save the day. But Seleucus' elephants were keeping Demetrius at bay, and Antigonus succumbed to his foes' javelins. Demetrius escaped to Greece, where he and his descendants would overcome and rule Macedonia for a century. Antigonus' hopes of restoring Alexander's empire died with him – fragmented beyond repair.

What happened to Macedonia? When Cassander died in 298 BCE, his young sons Antipater and Alexander V co-ruled for three years with their mother as regent until Antipater murdered their mother and took sole control of the throne. Alexander asked Demetrius to intervene, but instead of aiding Alexander, he murdered him, seizing Macedonia for himself. But then a coalition force of Lysimachus, Seleucus, and Ptolemy attacked Demetrius' holdings in Asia, taking Anatolia, Cilicia, Cyprus, and Lycia.

To make matters worse for Demetrius, Lysimachus and King Pyrrhus of Epirus ejected him from Macedon, dividing the country between them. Demetrius headed east in 287 BCE to retake his territories in Asia. The following year, however, Seleucus captured him, and he died in captivity. The alliance between Lysimachus and Pyrrhus collapsed with Lysimachus taking all of Macedon.

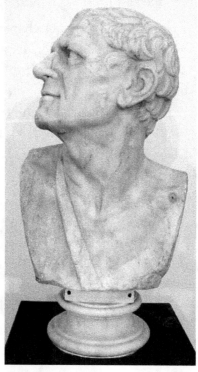

This marble bust of Lysimachus is a Roman copy of the Greek original.

https://en.wikipedia.org/wiki/Lysimachus#/media/File:Lisimaco_(c.d.),_copia_aug ustea_(23_ac-14_dc)_da_orig._del_II_sec_ac._6141.JPG

Meanwhile, in Egypt, Ptolemy decided to pass over his oldest son Ptolemy Ceraunus (Keraunos). He named his younger son from another wife, Ptolemy II, as his successor, so Ptolemy Ceraunus came to Lysimachus' court in Macedon. In 281 BCE, Lysimachus' one-time ally Seleucus invaded Lysimachus' territory in Asia Minor, and Lysimachus was killed in the Battle of

Corupedium. Seleucus was now the only general left who had fought with Alexander the Great, but he didn't last long. In the same year, Ptolemy Ceraunus, who was planning to usurp his empire, assassinated him. The last of the *Diadochi* (successors) of Alexander the Great was dead.

Seleucus' army stationed in Thrace proclaimed Ptolemy Ceraunus king; he forfeited any claim to Egypt's throne. Lysimachus' widow Arsinoe, daughter of Egypt's pharaoh, was Ptolemy Ceraunus' half-sister. Ceraunus asked Arsinoe – his half-sister – to marry him; despite their Macedonian heritage, they had assimilated the Egyptian custom of brother-sister marriages in the royal line. Arsinoe accepted his proposal, with the promise that her three sons by Lysimachus would be unharmed.

Unhappy in the marriage, Arsinoe began to plot against her half-brother-husband with her sons. When Ceraunus found out, he killed her two younger sons, but the oldest son escaped. Arsinoe returned to Egypt and married her full brother Ptolemy II, becoming both his queen and co-Pharoah.

Ptolemy Ceraunus' reign over Macedonia ended abruptly when a barbarian horde from the north suddenly invaded the country. A massive surge of 300,000 Celtic tribes spilled into Italy, Illyria, and Asia Minor. The Volcae tribe of southern Gaul overwhelmed Macedon in 279 BCE. The Celts made diplomatic overtures to Ceraunus, which he disregarded. He also turned down help from the Dardanians and launched an attack on the Celts before his whole army assembled.

The Gauls captured and decapitated him, mounting his head on a spear. After crushing Ceraunus' army, the Celts moved south to plunder other parts of Greece. In the chaos that followed Ceraunus' death, his brother Meleager took the throne, but after two months, the Macedonian military forced him to give up his crown.

Anarchy reigned for two years with multiple contenders for the throne. Finally, Demetrius' son Antigonus Gonatas allied with other Greeks to stop the Gaul's advance at Thermopylae and Delphi, forcing them into retreat. In 279 BCE, he ambushed the Gauls in Thrace, soundly defeating them, sending them out of Thrace and Macedonia and into Asia. Antigonus Gonatas ruled Macedonia for 33 years, restoring a measure of order to the war-torn country.

Chapter 14: Mainland Greece: The Last Embers

"Beautiful is the bloom of youth, but it lasts only for a fleeting time."

~Theocritus

An energetic new culture emerged in the Hellenistic era, blending Greek philosophy, science, math, and art with Egyptian, Indian, and Persian influences. The Archaic and Classical periods saw Athens, Sparta, Corinth, Thebes, and other city-states of mainland Greece reign as the military powerhouses and cultural centers of the known world. But in the Hellenistic Age, the large Hellenistic kingdoms held the military power, and the new centers of art and science were in Egypt's Alexandria and Seleucid Syria's Antioch.

So how did the ancient Greek cities, like Athens and Sparta, stay relevant? Did they even survive? With all the development of the eastern Greek world, what about the west? How did the Greek city-states of Italy and Sicily fare? This chapter will explore the outcomes of Sparta's social and agricultural reforms, the new Greek leagues and their role in Greece's affairs, and finally, the pyrrhic victories of King Pyrrhus of Epirus in his attempts to protect the city-states of Italy and Sicily.

Sparta was dying a slow death; it would fade into oblivion if something didn't happen quickly. Sparta's citizen population had seriously dwindled – over two-thirds of the men died in battle, and the rest weren't siring many children. For centuries, all Sparta's able-bodied, land-owning male citizens ages 20 to 60 served as full-time soldiers. When they weren't on military campaigns, the young men lived in the barracks instead of with their wives. Sparta's rigid social and governmental structures spelled its doom in the rapidly changing Greek world.

Spartan men spent most of their lives away in battle or at home in the barracks.

https://commons.wikimedia.org/wiki/File:Crat%C3%A8reVixD%C3%A9tail1.jpg

In 245 BCE, Agis IV came to the throne. He only ruled four years, but he spearheaded necessary reforms addressing Sparta's domestic crisis. Sparta citizens had once followed a simple "Spartan" lifestyle in an egalitarian system where each Spartan family held an equal land allotment. Now, only a few families owned most of the land, and they lived in luxury, while the rest were drowning in debt.

If a Spartan family had more than one son, they had to divide the farmland between the sons, and the smaller size of a farm would make it difficult for the sons to feed their families and their comrades in the barracks (the military men took turns hosting dinner each night). Or one son would get the land, and the others would be pauper outcastes – if they had no land, they couldn't serve in the military, and if they couldn't be in the military, what was the point of being Spartan?

King Agis' strategy to rectify the disparity among Sparta's families included forgiving all debt and repartitioning the agricultural land, so every family had an equal-sized farm. To address the shortage of farmers and soldiers, he looked at the Perioikoi non-citizens (immigrants to Sparta from other places) who were merchants, craftsmen, and manufacturers. They hadn't been fighting in the wars, so their population had grown while the Spartans were shrinking. Agis wanted all able-bodied Perioikoi men to serve as soldiers, owning a farm like the Spartan citizens.

King Agis presented his plan to the council, but Sparta still had two kings, and the other king, Leonidas, had grown up reveling in luxury at Seleucus II's court in Persia. The ordinary citizens and Perioikoi embraced Agis' plan, but the wealthy landowners were not about to part with their land. Unwilling to lose his lands and riches, he influenced the council against Agis – who lost by only one vote.

To get rid of his co-ruler, King Agis reminded the council that King Leonidas was more Persian than Spartan with his opulent lifestyle and Persian wife (marrying a foreigner went against Spartan law) and was rejecting Spartan ways. He successfully convinced the council to depose Leonidas, whose Spartan son-in-law Cleombrotus became king in his place – a man who shared Agis's values.

Still lacking the council's robust support, Agis postponed land redistribution and started with canceling the debts. With that settled, he left for war against the Aetolian League. But in his absence, Leonidas snuck back into Sparta, staged a coup, and usurped his throne. Cleombrotus escaped into exile, but Agis was strangled to death after a mock trial in 214 BCE.

After Agis' hasty execution, Leonidas' son Cleomenes returned from hunting to see the city being decorated for a wedding. "Who's getting married?" he asked his father.

"You are! To Agiatis."

Agiatis was King Agis' beautiful and exceptionally wealthy widow. Cleomenes guessed his father wanted control of her fortune but wondered how marriage would work out with the widow of a man killed by his father. As it turned out, Agiatis had been an ardent supporter of her first husband's reforms, and she quickly convinced an initially skeptical Cleomenes that he should finish the task Agis had started.

King Cleomenes III implemented the reforms King Agis envisioned. https://commons.wikimedia.org/wiki/File:Cleomenes_III.jpg

When Cleomenes III became king, he continued King Agis' reforms – beginning with his own property. He handed his land to the state for redistribution, and his family and friends followed his example, and eventually all the land-holders. He redivided all the land equally between 4000 citizens. Only about 2000 of the citizens were of Spartan ancestry – showing how drastic the population decline was. The rest were the Perioikoi, along with some mercenaries who had fought with the Spartans. All 4000 men trained as hoplites in the Spartan army. Cleomenes updated the Spartan military tactics and weaponry – training his men with the sarissa.

Cleomenes' reforms returned Sparta to its egalitarian origins and sparked reform in other city-states. However, while he temporarily increased the male citizen population by including the Perioikoi and mercenaries, he did not deal with the root causes of Sparta's population decline. Aristotle called it the *oliganthropia*: losing men in battle, a low fertility rate, and only allowing land-holders to serve in the military. Cleomenes suffered a devasting loss in the 222 BCE Battle of Sellasia against Macedon. His phalanx – most of Sparta's male citizens – was wiped out and Sparta was doomed. Cleomenes fled to Egypt and committed suicide.

For survival in the Hellenistic Age, independent city-states had two choices: ally with one of the large Hellenistic kingdoms or join a league. Antipater had thoroughly pummeled Athens in the Lamian War and garrisoned their port with Macedonian troops. To rid themselves of the Macedonians, Athens allied with Hellenistic Egypt, but that didn't go well. Despite Egypt's funding and Ptolemy's fleets, Macedonia's Antigonus Gonatas regained control in the Chremonidean War (267-261 BCE).

Other Greek city-states formed *Sympoliteia* or leagues to protect themselves, with the Aetolian and Achaean the most prominent. The Aetolian League, established in 370 BCE, controlled most of central Greece except Attica and Boeotia. It allied with Athens in the Lamian War and continued to resist Macedonian control during the Wars of the Diadochi. In 301 BCE, it gained control of Delphi, successfully defending Apollo's sanctuary from the Celtic invasion in 279 BCE. The following year, the Aetolian League took control of the critical Thermopylae Pass.

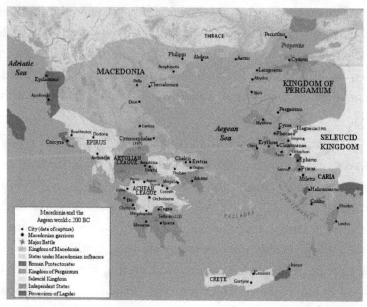

This map of Greece in the Hellenistic world depicts the Achaean and Aetolian Leagues.
https://en.wikipedia.org/wiki/Aetolian_League#/media/File:Macedonia_and_the_Aegean_World_c.200.png

In the Macedonian Wars, the Aetolian League was the Roman Republic's first Greek ally. After the wars, the Aetolian League allied with Antiochus III of the Seleucid Empire against Rome in the Roman-Syrian War, concerned about Rome's increasing power over the Greek world. The defeat of the Seleucid Empire was catastrophic for the Aetolian League – it was no longer strong enough to stand against Rome or have any military consequence.

In the fifth century BCE, an earthquake and tsunami destroyed the Achaean League's central city of Helike, but the Achaean League was reestablished in 280 BCE. The new Achaean League swiftly grew to encompass most of the Peloponnese except Sparta. In a daring night attack, the Achaean League successfully ejected the Macedonians from the Peloponnese and "freed" Corinth in 243 BCE – making it part of the league.

However, when the Achaean League fought against the Spartan King Cleomenes III (the reformer), they asked Macedonia to help. Although they crushed the Spartans, the Achaeans ended up enduring Macedonian control over the Peloponnese once again. In the Second Macedonian War, the Achaean League fought the Aetolian League in the Social War but pragmatically joined with the Aetolian League and Rome – the rising power – in the Second Macedonian War, breaking Macedonia's control over Greece, defeating Sparta, and taking over the entire Peloponnese.

In the Third Macedonian War (171-168 BCE), the Achaean League fell out with Rome, and in 146 BCE, Rome conquered the Achaeans at the Battle of Corinth, dissolving the League. In addition to the Aetolian and Achaean Leagues, the Northern League included the Asia Minor cities of Byzantium, Heraclea Pontica, Chalcedon, and Tium. The Cyclades formed the Nesiotic League. In the *Sympoliteia* system, the city-states had autonomy over local affairs, with a central league government over their collective military. They also used the same currency and measurements.

Everyone loves to win, but a *pyrrhic victory* is so costly it's not worth winning. That was the experience of King Pyrrhus of Epirus, who got involved with the *Magna Graecia* – the coastal Greek city-states of southern Italy – against Rome in the Pyrrhic War (280-275 BCE). After his first victory, he lamented, "If we win another such battle against the Romans, we will be completely lost."

It all started when ten Roman ships entered the Greek-controlled Gulf of Taranto (at the very bottom of Italy). Tarentum – a Spartan colony on the Gulf – had grown into the most important Greek city-state in Italy and one of the largest cities in the world. The enraged

Tarentines' formidable navy sank four Roman ships and captured a fifth. They then ejected Rome's garrison in Thurii.

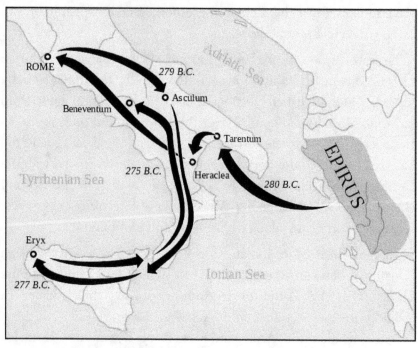

This map shows Pyrrhus' route from Epirus to Italy, then to Sicily and back. By Piom, translation by Pamela Butler - Image:Pyrrhic_War_Italy_PioM.svg, in Polish, CC BY-SA 3.0, https://commons.wikimedia.org/w/index.php?curid=4588930

Rome declared war on Tarentum, so the Greeks called on King Pyrrhus – they had helped him conquer Corfu, so it was his turn to return the favor. Pyrrhus was a cousin of Alexander the Great and had visions of building his own empire – if he helped Tarentum, he would get a foothold in Italy. Pyrrhus borrowed mercenaries, money, elephants, and horses from his brother-in-law Ptolemy II of Egypt, then sailed to southern Italy in 280 BCE with 25,000 soldiers. Meanwhile, an army of 30,000 Roman soldiers marched south toward Tarentum.

Pyrrhus quickly realized the Tarentines were happy to let him do the arduous work of defeating Rome while they enjoyed their baths and reveled at their festivals. Pyrrhus sternly prohibited frivolous pastimes and rounded up the men for military service. Long separated from their Spartan roots, many men left Tarentine, not accustomed to such austerity.

Hearing the Romans were rapidly approaching, Pyrrhus marched out to meet them at the Siris River, vexed that the Greek allies hadn't arrived. After observing the Roman camp from a high bluff – noting their discipline – he reflected, "These barbarians aren't barbarous; we shall see what they amount to." (The Greeks called all non-Greeks "barbarian," considering them uncivilized).

And indeed, he did see. In the Battle of Heraclea, Pyrrhus lined his troops along the river, which the Romans would have to forge before attacking. He opened with a cavalry charge, which initially broke the Roman lines, yet he'd never encountered such a strong, disciplined army. Unnerved, Pyrrhus quickly changed armor with his lieutenant – who was subsequently targeted and killed.

Pyrrhus' war elephants saved the day. The Romans had never fought elephants – their infantry cowered, and their horses stampeded off the field. But one wounded elephant panicked and charged back toward Pyrrhus' forces, crushing his men. The victory went to the Greeks, but both sides suffered colossal losses – up to 15,000 Romans and 13,000 Greeks died – almost half of both armies, but Rome had a ready supply of more troops, while Pyrrhus did not.

Pyrrhus spent the winter reinforcing his troops with his Macedonian and Ionian allies. In 279 BCE, he confronted Rome with 40,000 soldiers – once again on the banks of a surging river. Who would cross the river? The Romans politely offered to stand down while Pyrrhus' men crossed, but Pyrrhus promised the Romans they could cross unmolested.

The Pyrrhic War was Rome's first encounter with war elephants.
https://upload.wikimedia.org/wikipedia/commons/d/da/Pyrrhus_and_his_Elepha
nts.gif

The battle raged for two days, but the Romans kept the fight in dense woods with uneven ground, preventing horse and elephant charges. Over the winter, they'd devised 300 ox-drawn anti-elephant wagons, bristling with spears, with small catapults hurtling projectiles. On the first day, the Romans prevailed, but on the second day, Pyrrhus brought out the elephants - having them skirt the wagons on each end. Even from afar, the Roman horses were terrified and stampeded into the forest once again. Technically, Pyrrhus won: Rome lost 7000 men - twice as many as the Greeks. But Pyrrhus was impaled by a javelin, most of his commanders had perished, and his Italian allies were fearful of Rome's wrath. Pyrrhus gasped, "One more victory like that, and we're finished!"

Nicias, a Greek soldier, treacherously went to the Romans and offered to assassinate Pyrrhus. The Roman consul Fabricius considered this an insult to Roman valor and alerted Pyrrhus, who flayed Nicias and used his skin to form straps for a chair. Meanwhile, Rome renewed an alliance with Carthage, hearing rumors Pyrrhus might engage in Sicily.

And Pyrrhus did indeed sail to Sicily when the Greek city-states there asked him to rid them of tyrants and defend them against Carthage - in exchange - he could be their king. Simultaneously, the Macedonians offered him their throne - the Celts had just decapitated their king Ptolemy Ceraunus. Pyrrhus chose Sicily with its proximity to Carthage, which he intended to conquer. Thus, Pyrrhus suddenly interrupted the war in Italy, exasperating the Tarentines but leaving the Romans chuckling. Now they had time to gain control over the rebel Italian tribes and conquer the Greek cities of Croton and Lokrami in southern Italy.

When Pyrrhus arrived in Sicily in 278 BCE, Carthage was already attacking Syracuse, and they quickly attacked him too! Pyrrhus only captured two cities - Panormus and Eryx - but abandoned Sicily after three years, realizing he was no match for Carthage. As his fleet disappeared over the horizon, Panormus and Eryx overthrew the garrisons he left behind. Pyrrhus arrived back in Tarentum with only 20,000 troops left - and with the Tarentines furious at him for leaving in the middle of things and allowing Rome to gain ground.

Pyrrhus still believed he could get a foothold in Italy. In his third attack, he led his army to Maleventum (meaning *ominous arrival*) to confront the Roman consul Curius. He planned to march through the night and launch a surprise attack in the morning. But his army got lost in the woods and separated – when they staggered out of the forest at Maleventum, weak and exhausted, they were at the top of a bluff, quickly spied by Curius' troops in the valley. So much for a surprise attack! It was indeed a "bad arrival!"

Curius charged, capturing some elephants and quickly routing the weary, dehydrated, disorganized Greeks. The Greeks did manage a charge with their remaining elephants, but the Romans had learned to deal with war elephants by piercing their sides with spears. The enraged elephants charged back through the Greek ranks in pain, creating pandemonium and crushing men. Not winning even a pyrrhic victory – Pyrrhus suffered a bitter defeat at Maleventum.

He made his way to Tarentum, then sailed back to Epirus. His parting gift to the Tarentines was the chair made from Nicias' skin. The Tarentines hoped he was gone for good – their situation with Rome was far worse than when Pyrrhus came to rescue them. The Greek city-states in Italy made peace with Rome and continued self-rule, but with a Roman garrison and Roman laws. Pyrrhus died three years later when an old lady on a rooftop in Argos threw a tile at him, hitting him in the neck and paralyzing him.

Chapter 15: The Dissemination of Hellenism

"Whenever Hellenes take anything from non-Hellenes,

they eventually carry it to a higher perfection."

~Plato, *Epinomis*

Alexander's spectacular ambitions encompassed more than military conquest of the known world. He had a keen interest in culture, and as he explored the eastern lands, he was intentional in syncretizing those cultures with Greek art, lifestyle, philosophy, and sciences. He established multiple cities as cultural centers, melding east and west. The Middle Eastern, Asian, and North African people adopted Greek ways, and the Greeks assimilated Asian, Middle Eastern, and Egyptian culture into a new, exciting Hellenistic civilization.

On the Nile Delta in Egypt, Alexandria grew into a premier center of trade and Hellenistic culture with an international population of over a half-million people. Its spacious harbor, over which the Pharos Lighthouse soared 350 feet high, hosted ships from around the Mediterranean, enabling thriving commerce. Alexandria had a museum with an art gallery, botanical gardens, an observatory, and a zoo. The Alexandrian Library held a treasure-trove of ancient literature – a half-million papyrus scrolls that gifted scholars could reference.

Hellenistic scholars were the world's primary source of scientific knowledge for centuries. Aristarchus of Samos was the first astronomer to theorize that the earth rotated on an axis once a day and revolved with other planets around the sun once a year. Unfortunately, his theory never caught on until Nicolaus Copernicus triggered an astronomical revolution eighteen centuries later. Many Hellenistic astronomists realized the earth was a sphere – not flat. Eratosthenes, the head of Alexandria's research library, used geometry to calculate the earth's circumference as 28,000 to 29,000 miles. Amazingly, he wasn't far off! Today's calculations say the distance around the planet is 24,901 miles.

The Hellenistic mathematician Archimedes of Syracuse enhanced the geometric approximations of the ancient Babylonians and Egyptians, correctly determining the ratio of a circle's circumference to its diameter: pi (π). Archimedes also explained how to move a heavy object with only a small amount of force. He taught the law of the lever, using geometric reasoning, and invented the first compound pulley. Plutarch reported that Archimedes demonstrated the compound pulley by moving a ship – by himself! Other Hellenistic scientists built on his concepts to develop a steam engine, force pump, and pneumatic machines.

People with nothing in common drew closer and thrived culturally through the Koine Greek language. The standard Koine dialect united Greeks and other ethnicities spread throughout Alexander's empire, enabling traders, travelers, and military men to communicate efficiently. It empowered scholars from far-flung regions to discuss philosophy, science, art, and religion.

Ptolemy II, the Macedonian Pharaoh of Egypt, commissioned 72 Jewish scholars to translate the Tanakh (Torah, Writings, and Prophets) into Koine Greek and place it in the Library of

Alexandria. Jews throughout the Greek world used this Septuagint translation. Jesus read from the Greek Septuagint in the synagogue (Luke 4:17-21), and this - more often than the Hebrew Tanakh (Old Testament) - is the translation he and his apostles quoted in their teachings and writings.

The apostles wrote the entire New Testament in Koine Greek - the lingua franca or common language of the Middle East, North Africa, and much of Europe. The Apostle Paul demonstrated a Hellenistic education by quoting from the Greek poets and philosophers Epimenides, Aratus, and Menander. When Paul and the other apostles traveled to Sicily, Corinth, Athens, Macedonia, and other destinations, they had a common Greek language, culture, and scripture - which enhanced the swift spread of Christianity among Jews and Greeks.

While the writings of Plato and Aristotle (tutor to Alexander the Great) continued to shape Hellenistic thinking, new philosophers appeared who led Hellenistic philosophy through several stages: reason, skepticism, and mysticism. They all concerned themselves with man's salvation from evil and hardship - more concerned with the individual's welfare than the good of society.

Epicurus of Athens taught the gods were disinterested in human affairs. Thus, humans should only consider what their five senses perceived - material things, not spiritual matters. We often think of Epicureans as pleasure lovers - especially enjoying excellent food. However, Epicurus warned against gluttony, advocating moderation in all aspects of life. Indulging physical desires is good but in moderation! Debauchery should be avoided since the excess of any pleasure brings pain.

Epicurus said ultimate pleasure is total serenity, which comes from eliminating mental pain. How? By ending fear - specifically fear of the gods. He said the gods could care less what's happening to humanity - they are only interested in grasping their own happiness. Epicurus said the gods don't punish or reward people in this life or the afterlife, so there is no reason to fear them.

Plato's school, the Platonic Academy, continued into the Hellenistic Age but developed his teachings in several different directions. Academic Skepticism, founded by Arcesilaus and developed further by Carneades, believed knowledge is unattainable. We only can know what we can perceive from our senses, but appearances are never what they seem. One's assumptions are always wrong. Truth exists, but we can't grasp it. However, one can be slightly wrong versus utterly wrong.

The Skeptics taught we have no definitive understanding of the spiritual world or life's meaning, nor can we judge what is good or evil. When we stop worrying about our morality or others – we can be happy. We shouldn't be obsessed with good and evil – we can't understand the world, so there's no use trying to reform it. Once we reach a state of detachment, we find serenity and satisfaction.

Neoplatonism or "Plotinism" – after its teacher Plotinus – took Plato's ideas in a mystical and spiritual direction. All things have their being in the One – the Good – the pinnacle of existence. Through purity and meditation, one's soul can rise to unite with the One – our goal in life.

When one's mind and body are in perfect harmony with one's soul – when one's soul governs the body, rather than the body ruling itself – all is well and reflects the upper world. When the soul is in unison with the One, then harmony with the body is achieved. When one's material body and desires govern a person, this leads to conflict and discord. Evil is the absence of light – the lack of complete goodness.

The Cynics also continued their teachings in the Hellenistic Period under Crates and Menippus. The core of Cynicism is living in purity and harmony with nature through strict discipline, rejecting riches and influence, and living simply, without possessions. Crates of Thebes renounced his inheritance to live as a pauper on Athens' streets.

He taught that we shouldn't be consumed with the love of money and craving wealth; we should be content with what we have. Crates said most people in the world are in a state of *tuphos* (mist, smoke) - the mental confusion that entraps people when their lives revolve around materialism. He taught that asceticism and contentment clear away the fog and made one fruitful and healthy.

Menippus, a freed slave who lived in Thebes, was another Cynic who wrote humorous yet biting satire. He taught that a person should be indifferent to life's circumstances and the judgments of others. One should love humanity and pursue virtue yet reject social conventions. Exercise - of both the mind and body - was intrinsic to mental and physical health.

Aristotle's philosophy was developed and maintained in the Peripatetic School, which stressed examining the world, beginning with the facts one can glean from experience. Philosophy is science, and one should learn through observation and inductive reasoning, always asking, "Why?" Two principal leaders of Aristotle's Peripatetic School were Theophrastus and Strato.

Theophrastus studied under Plato and Aristotle and presided over the Peripatetic School for 36 years. His primary interests were biology (he studied botany and wrote two books on plants), ethics, physics, and metaphysics (philosophy dealing with identity, mind and matter, space and time, and cause and effect). He was a vegetarian because he believed animals could feel and reason like humans, so it was unjust to take their lives.

He authored a small book called *Characters* - vignettes of different personality types who walked the streets of Athens. Some were vulgar, some were simpletons, and some were uncultured. He profiled the arrogant person, the busybody, the complainer, the tactless person, the messy person, the flatterer, the social climber, the talker, and the obnoxious exhibitionist. Even today, one can chuckle at his humorous sketches, recognizing the characters he discusses.

Strato studied at the Peripatetic School in Athens, then went to Egypt to tutor Ptolemy II and the brilliant astronomer Aristarchus, returning to Athens to direct the Peripatetic school after Theophrastus' death. Strato concentrated on natural science, holding a secular worldview unconcerned with morality, believing that any divine entity exists only as an unconscious force in nature. He stressed meticulous research - using the example of pouring water to demonstrate that falling objects accelerate.

In the Hellenistic Age, a new school of philosophy appeared called Stoicism, founded by Zeno of Citium. Stoicism had its foundations in Cynicism, stressing that peace comes from living pure lives in tune with nature. Zeno met Crates in Athens and became his pupil. Stoicism flourished as a significant philosophical school during the Hellenistic Age and continued through the Roman era.

Zeno taught that God has set up natural laws which run the universe, and people need to live ethical lives in unity with others and in agreement with God's will. He cautioned that desire for wealth and power were dangerous distractions from harmony with God. Zeno said we should focus on what we can control and not worry about the rest. He believed logic was imperative for avoiding deception.

Zeno said the path to actual knowledge leads through four stages: perception, assent, comprehension, and knowledge. He believed God was a reasoning Being - a divine fire - to whom all things belong, including individual souls. Happiness comes through reason that connects to the *Logos* (spiritual logic) that governs everything, from which springs virtue. Living according to reason rather than impulse and passion is what separates us from animals. Virtue is diametrically opposed to vice, which is the result of rejecting logic.

Various art forms flourished in the Hellenistic period, most notably sculpture. While Classical Age sculptures portrayed serene, idealized forms with perfect bodies and faces, the Hellenistic sculptures were more realistic, including ordinary people in natural poses: wrinkles, warts, and all. The Hellenistic sculptures captured extremes of emotion and expressive movement.

Horror and agony are graphically portrayed in the Laocoön Group sculpture.

https://commons.wikimedia.org/wiki/File:Laocoon_Pio-Clementino_Inv1059-1064-1067.jpg

The *Laocoön Group* features the Trojan priest Laocoön and his two sons in a deathly struggle. Laocoön had warned the people to burn the Trojan horse, which, unknown to the Trojans, was full of Greek warriors. Fighting for the Greeks, the goddess Athena retaliated by sending deadly sea serpents to strangle and kill Laocoön and his sons. The sculpture grotesquely portrays struggling bodies and the raw emotion of horror. The statue was unearthed in Rome in 1506 and placed in the Vatican, where it is still. Michelangelo described it as a "miracle of art" and strove to emulate its passion and movement in his own art.

The Colossus of Rhodes was the most massive statue of the Hellenistic Age. The 108-foot-high bronze and iron sculpture of the sun-god Helios towered over Rhodes' harbor, celebrating the city's victory over a siege by the Macedonian King Demetrius Poliorcetes. One of the seven wonders of the ancient world, it was toppled by an earthquake in 226 BCE, broken off at the knees, and lay there for 800 years until the Muslims captured Rhodes and melted the sculpture down.

An exhausted Hercules (Heracles) leans on his club, draped with the Nemean Lion's skin, killed in the first of his labors.

https://en.wikipedia.org/wiki/Farnese_Hercules

The Farnese Hercules (*Hercules de Farnesio*) sculpture was initially cast in bronze but then melted down by the Crusaders during the 1205 CE Sack of Constantinople. A marble copy was made, which is what can be seen today in Naples. The statue depicts the weary hero Hercules, having just completed the last of the *12 Labors* in penance for killing his wife and children while driven mad by his goddess stepmother Hera who kept trying to kill him.

The Venus de Milo sculpture was painted, and she wore bracelets and other jewelry.

https://commons.wikimedia.org/wiki/File:Venus_de_Milo_-_Front.jpeg

The captivating Venus de Milo sculpture represents the Greek goddess of love Aphrodite (called Venus by the Romans) posed in a sinuous curve. Found on the island of Milos in 1820, she is the epitome of feminine grace and youthful beauty.

The Winged Victory of Samothrace represents the dynamic celebration of triumph.
https://commons.wikimedia.org/wiki/File:Winged_Victory_of_Samothrace_(Pushkin_State_Museum_of_Fine_Arts).jpg

Another Hellenistic sculptural masterpiece found at Rhodes was the *Nike* (winged victory) of Samothrace, which now graces the Daru staircase in the Louvre. Sculpted from Paros marble, she is a compelling image of the goddess of victory in flight. Her clothing ripples as if caught in the sea breeze, clinging to her belly and thighs as if wet.

The colors of the Stag Hunt floor mosaic are reminiscent of red on black Greek pottery.

https://commons.wikimedia.org/wiki/File:Deer_hunt_mosaic_from_Pella.jpg

Mosaics increased in popularity in the Hellenistic Age, with *tesserae* (small cubes) of glass or stone formed into elaborate pictures. Many mosaics have been found in homes of the period, showing the increased wealth of the Hellenistic era. The intense drama and violent movement of the *Stag Hunt* mosaic from Pella, Macedonia, is similar in composition and color to the *Lion Hunt* mosaic (pictured in chapter 13), also from Pella. Signed by the artist Gnosis, it likely represents Alexander the Great with his dog Peritas.

The *Alexander Mosaic* (or *Battle of Issus Mosaic*) was constructed in the House of the Faun in Pompeii but is a copy of an earlier Greek painting. Measuring 12 by 17 feet, it is now in the Naples National Archaeological Museum. It depicts the struggle between Darius III of Persia and Alexander the Great in the Battle of Issus. Two sections of this mosaic – Darius III and Alexander – are pictured in chapter 12 of this book.

Like the Hellenistic sculptures and mosaics, the architecture of this era was dramatic, elaborate, and often massive. King Attalos II of Pergamon built the marble and limestone Stoa of Attalos as a gift to Athens. An ancient shopping center with spectacular architecture located in the Agora (public space), two floors each hosted 21 shops behind a covered colonnade. The Stoa was rebuilt in the 1950s, using original remains when possible and imitating the ancient architecture.

The Temple of Trajan in the Pergamon Acropolis overlooks the city. https://commons.wikimedia.org/wiki/File:Pergamon_-_02.jpg

Pergamon, in present-day Turkey, was a major cultural center that reached its apex in the Hellenistic Age. The city's acropolis was built on an 1100-foot mesa, modeled after Athens' acropolis. The dramatic temples and theaters are visible from anywhere in the city. The temple of Trajan and the Temple of Athena have been partially reconstructed following the original architecture, using the remnants of the ancient buildings when possible.

The Hellenistic world began declining by 150 BCE. Rome was becoming stronger as the Hellenistic city-states and countries grew weaker. Rome would soon expand into an empire that would encompass much of Greek territory. However, Rome championed, imitated, and preserved Greek culture – notably its architecture, drama, philosophy, sculptures, and politics.

Chapter 16: The Rise of Rome

"They told me, Heraclitus, they told me you were dead.

They brought me bitter news to hear and bitter tears to shed.

I wept, as I remembered, how often you and I

Had tired the sun with talking and sent him down the sky."

˜ Callimachus, *Elegy to Heraclitus*

As the sun rose over Rome, it set on Greece. Many great warriors have fought in spectacular battles since the dawn of time, but Rome's epic conquest of Greece changed the course of history. After Rome conquered the ancient tribes surrounding Rome, it brazenly expanded southward. Shortly after the end of the wars with Pyrrhus, all the Greek city-states of southern Italy had surrendered to Rome. Now, Rome desired control of the strategic island of Sicily with its wealthy Greek cities, just two miles across the strait from the toe of Italy's boot. From there, Rome moved to the conquest of Macedonia and the other great Greek kingdoms and leagues.

An alliance with savage pirates got Rome involved with Sicily and the First Punic War against Carthage. Italian mercenaries called Mamertines had taken over the city of Messana (Messina), killing all the men and keeping the young women as their wives. They transformed peaceful Messana into their base for ruthless pirate raids around Sicily. Hiero II, the tyrant ruler of the fantastically wealthy Greek city of Syracuse south of Messana, grew exasperated with the Mamertine desperados disrupting his trade and ravaging the coastline for 20 years. Around 270 BCE, he marched toward Messana, successfully fighting Mamertine pirates along the way.

A Carthaginian fleet had moored in Messana's harbor, and the Mamertines called on them for help. Hiero withdrew, not wanting to fight Carthage. He attacked Messana again four years later, and this time Messana called on Rome for help. The Romans' eagerness to stop Carthage's power expansion in the region took precedence over their reservations against joining forces with pirates. Rome came to Messana's aid, sending 16,000 troops to Sicily – the first time the Roman military had fought outside Italy's peninsula. The alarmed Hiero asked Carthage for protection – which didn't help, as Rome soundly defeated the Syracusan-Carthaginian coalition.

Hieron surrendered and allied with Rome, enabling him to stay in power. Rome then brutally attacked the Greek city of Acragas, enslaving its population, impelling other Greek cities of Sicily to ally with Rome, leading to an all-out war between Rome and Carthage. Rome carried off the astounding feat of building 100 large quinquereme warships and 20 triremes in two months to take on Carthage's legendary navy!

Rome immediately scored brilliant victories against Carthage at sea and land, winning the largest naval battle in history at the Battle of Cape Ecnomus – involving 330 ships. But then things went horribly wrong. Rome attacked the city of Carthage, which allied with Sparta and fought back with 100 war elephants, killing 12,000 Romans. The Romans who escaped met ran into a horrific storm that sank most of their ships and drowned 100,000 men in the worst shipwreck event of history.

The survivors limped into Sicily, but in indomitable Roman fashion, captured the Greek city of Palermo, selling everyone into slavery who couldn't pay a 200-drachmas fee. Fighting continued between Carthage and Rome, with Sicily's Greek city-states caught in the middle. Finally, after two decades, Rome prevailed, winning the First Punic War, forcing Carthage to withdraw entirely from Sicily. Rome had its first offshore province, and the Greeks of Sicily now came under Roman rule.

While fighting Hannibal's unexpected invasion of northern Italy via the Alps from France, Rome was simultaneously embroiled in heated wars against the Greeks. Complicated politics drove the Macedonian Wars as Rome struggled with the Greek empires and leagues, fighting on Greece's mainland for the first time. Rome portrayed itself as the "deliverer" of the Greek people from Macedonian domination.

Philip V of Macedonia fought Rome in two wars, his son Perseus in a third.

https://commons.wikimedia.org/wiki/File:Philip_V_of_Macedon_BM.jpg

King Philip V of Macedonia sent his envoys to Hannibal of Carthage, who was in Italy wreaking havoc on Rome's water sources, food stores, transportation venues, and weapon manufacturing. Philip was angry at Rome's interference in neighboring Epirus and Illyria, which he intended to take for himself, so he allied with Hannibal to fight Rome. Philip's envoys slipped into Italy to negotiate the treaty but got caught on their way out, and Rome got the treaty scroll, which alerted them to keep a close eye on Philip.

While Rome was enduring Hannibal's scorched earth tactics, Philip lay siege to Apollonia in Illyria in 214 BCE. But Rome sent reinforcements, and Philip had to retreat. Philip successfully took two Illyrian fortresses, inducing Rome to ally with the Aetolian League against Macedonia. The Aetolians supplied soldiers, and Rome sent 25 warships.

The Aetolian League launched a siege against Acarnania in central Greece – Philip's ally. Sending their wives and children to Epirus, the Acarnanians fought valiantly against the Aetolians. They were winning until Rome's navy captured several of their coastal cities and gave them to the League. The joint Roman-Aetolian forces conquered Anticyra in 211 BCE; Philip was able to take it back, but not before the population had been sold into slavery.

Philip allied with Bithynia (in Turkey) to push the Aetolian League out of Thessaly. At this point, Sparta entered the war, joining with Rome and the Aetolian League against Macedonia and her allies. In 209 BCE, Philip's daunting Macedonian-Bithynian coalition defeated Sparta and the Aetolian League in the Peloponnese. The Aetolian League was at the point of making peace with Philip when the Roman fleet sailed into the Gulf of Corinth. But Philip brought the Romans to their knees in a stunning victory at Sicyon in the Peloponnese – then rushed home to defend Macedonia against a Dardanian invasion.

The Dying Gaul sculpture represents Attalus I's defeat of the Celtic Galatians. https://en.wikipedia.org/wiki/Attalus_I#/media/File:Dying_gaul.jpg

Philip had a menacing foe in King Attalus I of Pergamon, champion of the Greeks against the unruly Celtic Galatians. Attalus had allied with the Aetolian League to check Philip's unbridled ambition. His navy patrolled the Aegean with Rome's fleets, hindering Philip's movements. Attalus narrowly escaped capture by Philip when the Macedonians slipped through the Thermopylae Pass. To Philip's relief, Attalus had to withdraw from the war to defend Pergamum against a Bithynian invasion.

Once Attalus's fleets left the region, Philip briskly captured several cities around the undefended Gulf of Corinth. Desperately needing more naval power against Carthage, Rome pulled its fleets out of the Aegean Sea, only patrolling the Adriatic – protecting its own coast and its trading centers. That left just the Spartans and the Aetolian League challenging Philip and his allies. Philopoemen of Megalopolis killed the Spartan commander Machanidas, putting

Sparta out of the war. Philip ejected the Aetolians from Thessaly and Ionia and razed their federation capital of Thermum.

Lacking support from Rome or other allies, the dejected Aetolian League surrendered. At that point, Rome suddenly decided to divert forces from their war with Carthage, sending 10,000 men and 1000 cavalry to Illyria, but it was too late. The Aetolian League no longer wanted to fight Philip. Rome's war with Carthage was ending, and Philip knew when that happened, Rome would be targeting him again, so while he was winning, he ended the First Macedonian War with the Peace of Phoenice Treaty in 205 BCE.

A secret plot to usurp Egypt's throne instigated the Second Macedonian War in 200 BCE; Ptolemy IV of Egypt had just died, leaving his six-year-old son Ptolemy V as Pharoah. Philip V and Antiochus the Great, ruler of the Seleucid Empire, schemed to overthrow vulnerable Egypt while the royal family wrestled over the regency. Antiochus would rule Egypt and Cyprus if the conspiracy worked, and Philip would take the Aegean Sea area and Cyrene.

Antiochus the Great of the Seleucid Empire allied with Philip to conquer Egypt.

https://commons.wikimedia.org/wiki/File:Antiochus_III_coin.JPG

Like the wind, Antiochus overcame Damascus, Sidon, and Samaria in Coele-Syria. Once again, the Aetolian League panicked and desperately begged Rome to help them fight Macedonia and

Antiochus. Philip sailed out to war, besieging Egypt's naval base in Samos and conquering Miletus in the Aegean. Meanwhile, Antiochus trounced the Anatolians, ending Egypt's rule over Judea, welcomed into Jerusalem by the cheering Jews. They had no clue that Antiochus' son would place Zeus' statue in their temple and defile it by sacrificing a pig.

Having just won its third and last Punic War against Carthage, Rome issued an ultimatum to Philip – stay in Macedonia and Thrace, leave the rest of Greece alone, and leave Egypt alone. Philip received Rome's order as he was besieging Abydos in the Dardanelles. He laughed and continued storming the city's walls. Almost the entire population met a violent death three days later when the walls fell. The enraged Roman Senate declared war against Philip.

The Roman Consul Sulpicius sailed with his troops to Epirus, engaging in a few quick skirmishes with Philip. Then Philip heard the Dardanians were encroaching on Macedonia's border again and slipped away with his army in the middle of the night. When the Romans woke up – the Macedonians had gone! Sulpicius raced to catch up with the Macedonians but finally returned to his fleet and began launching assaults on Philip's naval bases.

In the following year, Rome's new consul Titus Quinctius Flamininus drove Philip out of most of Greece, then launched an unexpected attack on Philip's rearguard in Albania, killing 2000 Macedonians. Another ghastly loss occurred at the Battle of Cynoscephalae in Thessaly in 197 BCE – a strange battle where nobody could see more than a few feet in front of them because dense fog filled the valley.

Consul Flamininus had 20 war elephants – the first time Rome had used elephants in battle. The confused and disoriented Macedonians retreated to the hills where visibility was better, but the Roman cavalry circled around and forced them back to the plain. Through the fog, the Macedonians heard the terrifying sound of trumpeting elephants and stomping feet echoing through the valley. Where were they? Suddenly, the elephants loomed out of the mist to the soldier's screams. By the time the sun burned away the fog, 8000 Macedonians lay dead. Philip had no choice but to surrender – with harsh terms: abandon all Greek territories he'd acquired, disband his navy and most of his army, and remain within his borders. The Second Macedonian War had concluded.

Five years later, the Aetolian League switched sides and fought against Rome and for Antiochus the Great for Thrace, which Antiochus had claimed. King Nabis of Sparta allied with the League, resentful of Rome stealing his coastal cities. Sparta reclaimed some of their coastal towns, but then the Achaean League of the Peloponnese initiated hostile actions against King Nabis, who called the Aetolian League for help.

The Aetolian League sent 1000 infantry and 300 cavalry to Sparta, but treachery was afoot. Instead of helping King Nabis fight the Achaean League, the Aetolians assassinated him! Antiochus arrived in Greece with his troops – too late to help Nabis – but he hammered the Achaean League until Rome swiftly responded with two legions that chased Antiochus out of Greece.

Macedonia's final challenge to Rome arose in the Third Macedonian War of 171 to 168 BCE. Philip had died, and his merciless and ambitious son Perseus had murdered his half-brother Demetrius and stolen the throne. While Perseus was negotiating a marriage alliance with the granddaughter of Antiochus the Great, the Sapaei tribe of Thrace, which had allied with Rome, suddenly attacked. Perseus successfully won back his gold mines, but now Rome was disgruntled because Perseus had defeated an ally.

Perseus allied with King Cotys IV, who ruled Thrace's largest state and lured other Greek states to pool their forces with him against Rome, vowing to restore Greece to its old glory days of power and wealth. Starry-eyed, many of the Greek city-states visualized Perseus as their savior from Rome who would bring back the prestige and strength they once wielded. But Macedonia's neighbor King Eumenes II of Pergamum headed to Rome, warning that Perseus was stockpiling weapons and forming war alliances, which triggered Rome to declare war on Macedonia.

Perseus triumphantly conquered northern Thessaly in 171 BCE, but then troops from Rome and Pergamon marched over steep mountains to confront Perseus at Larissa in Thessaly. Although Perseus withdrew in the Battle of Callinicus, he claimed the victory for Macedon, as his army killed 2000 of the Roman forces while only losing 400 of his own.

Not long after, the hungry Romans were out harvesting the grain ripening in the countryside, leaving their camp with only a small guard. Perseus raided the camp while they were away, capturing the 600 Romans guarding the camp along with the Romans' supplies. But the Roman commander Publius Licinius was nearby. He viciously attacked Perseus, trapping his men in a narrow pass; in the fierce battle, Macedonia lost 8000 men, and 4000 Romans died.

Perseus was Macedonia's last king.

https://commons.wikimedia.org/wiki/File:Macedonia_-_king_Perseus_-_179-178_BC_-_silver_tetradrachm_-_head_of_king_Perseus_-_eagle_-_M%C3%BCnchen_GL.jpg

Rome's astute new commander Aemilius Paullus crushingly defeated Perseus at the Battle of Pydna on Macedonia's shore in 168 BCE. The spineless Perseus fled the field, abandoning his men to the Romans, who killed 20,000 Macedonians and captured 11,000. Paullus' plunder of Perseus' riches allowed a sizeable tax break for Rome's grateful citizens. The Romans tracked Perseus to Samothrace, where the islanders gave him up.

His captors dragged Perseus, Macedonia's last king, in chains through Rome's streets at the head of a splendid triumph (victory parade). Carrying war trophies and displaying Perseus' chariot, exhilarated Roman troops wearing laurel wreaths and even elephants paraded through Rome to the cheers of a jubilant crowd. Perseus was imprisoned in Rome until he died. Rome partitioned his kingdom of Macedonia into four republics, avoiding future unification by banning trade and intermarriage between the provinces.

Two decades later, the Achaean League made a suicidal declaration of war on Rome – their former ally. They were still nursing a grudge because Rome had taken League members hostage during the Third Macedonian War to ensure they wouldn't ally with Macedonia. The Achaeans also nurtured ambitions to expand their territory, which Rome forbade. Instead, Rome demanded the League retreat to their original cities.

The Romans swiftly decimated the Achaean's main force led by General Critolaos, who did not anticipate the Roman consul Mummius' brilliant maneuvers. At Scarpheia, most of the losing Achaean soldiers committed suicide – those who didn't were captured or killed. General Critolaos disappeared without a trace. Many Achaean League towns at once surrendered, but the rest of the League rallied around General Diaeus at Corinth.

The Battle of Leukopetra at Corinth was disastrous for the Achaean League. In just a few hours, the Romans overcame the Greeks. Diaeus escaped to Arcadia and committed suicide. For three days, the Romans waited to enter the city, wary of an ambush. Most Corinthians snuck away, but the Romans massacred all the men who remained and captured the women and children as slaves. Then Rome burned the great city of Corinth after plundering its precious sculptures and artwork, which were taken to Rome but suffered much damage in the chaos.

Corinth lay desolate until Julius Caesar rebuilt it in 44 BCE. The fateful battle at Corinth marked the beginning of Roman domination throughout mainland Greece. With the Achaean League now dissolved, the rest of Greece crumbled. For the next 100 years, Greece and the eastern Mediterranean experienced continuous shifting of alliances, no longer the dominant world powers. Yet Greece exerted persevering cultural influence over Rome, which assimilated Greek art, literature, philosophy, and political science - spreading it throughout its bourgeoning empire.

Chapter 17: The Fall of the Hellenistic Kingdoms

"Those who believe that the world of being is governed by luck or chance

and that it depends upon material causes

are far removed from the divine and the notion of the One."

~ Plotinus, *Ennead VI, Books 6-9*

Fierce internecine strife in Rome and Cleopatra's love affairs with Julius Caesar and Mark Antony complicated the Roman Republic's efforts to gain control of Alexander the Great's former Greek empire. Although Rome took control of the Greek peninsula in 146 BCE, it continued fighting the Greek kingdoms in Asia Minor, the Middle East, and Africa for the next century until they fell, one by one, ending with Egypt in 31 BCE. Although Egypt's fall marked the end of the Hellenistic Age, Koine Greek continued as the principal language in the Eastern Roman Empire for the next three centuries.

While the Diadochi Wars were raging, General Lysimachus kept his immense treasury at the mountainous city of Pergamon (Pergamum) in what is now eastern Turkey. The city of Pergamon was a Greek city under Persian control, liberated by Alexander the Great. When Lysander became king of neighboring Thrace, he appointed his lieutenant Philetaerus as Pergamon's governor, who enlarged the town.

The Temple of Trajan stood on Pergamon's acropolis.

Photo by Carlos Delgado; CC-BY-SA

https://commons.wikimedia.org/wiki/File:Pergamon_-_04.jpg

When Lysimachus died in the 281 BCE Battle of Corupedium, Pergamon became an independent city, with Philetaerus as its ruler and founder of the Attalid dynasty (named after his father, Attalus). Philetaerus quickly acquired the surrounding land, turning Pergamon into a city-state, and built palaces and temples on the stunning acropolis towering over the city.

Due to an unfortunate accident in infancy that damaged his testicles, Philetaerus never married or had children. His nephew and heir Eumenes enlarged Pergamon's territory into a small kingdom. Eumenes' cousin Attalus I (Attalus the Great) was the first to take the title of king after conquering the Celtic Galatians, who'd been rampaging through Asia Minor.

Pergamon metamorphosized into a powerful kingdom and cultural center under the Attalid dynasty and became Rome's loyal supporter. Pergamon allied with Rome against Philip V in the First and Second Macedonian Wars and against the Seleucid King Antiochus III, rewarded by Rome in 188 BCE with most of the one-time Seleucid provinces in Asia Minor.

Rome had an eerie religious problem in 205 BCE, with meteor showers and other phenomena frightening the population. After scholars perused the ancient *Sibylline Books* of prophecies, they found an oracle saying that a foreigner warring against Italy could be defeated if the Mother Goddess came to Rome. Obviously, the foreigner was Hannibal of Carthage, who had been in a bitter war against Rome for years.

The Romans believed their Mother Goddess lived on Mount Ida in northwestern Turkey, overlooking the ruins of Troy – their ancestral home. Rome sent a delegation to their old friend King Attalus, asking for help. He gave them the sacred uncarved stone of black meteorite, which the local people called *Cybele* or "the Mother of the Gods." The delegates carried it back to Rome, where they called her *Magna Mater* (Great Mother).

Queen Stratonice, the wife of Attalus' son and successor Eumenes II, married four times – twice to Eumenes II and twice to his brother Attalus II. King Eumenes had gone to Rome to warn about Perseus stockpiling weapons for war in Macedonia. On his way back, he was attacked, and the fake news arrived in Pergamon that King Eumenes was dead. So, Attalus took the throne and married his brother's widow.

Only Eumenes wasn't dead – just injured. After he recovered, he returned to Pergamon, where a sheepish Attalus handed back his crown . . . and his wife. Despite the awkward situation, Eumenes and Attalus were cordial and cooperative. Together, they built Pergamon to its apex, modeling it after Athens. Eumenes and Stratonice had one son, Attalus III. When Eumenes died in 159

BCE (this time for real), Attalus III was only eleven - too young to rule.

Attalus II Philadelphos (brother loving) founded the cities of Philadelphia and Attalia.
https://commons.wikimedia.org/wiki/File:II._Attalos_Heykeli_detay.JPG

Attalus II married Stratonice . . . again and took the throne as his nephew's regent. He reigned for 21 years - never giving the throne to Attalus III when he came of age. Attalus III didn't seem to mind - he had scant interest in ruling even after Attalus II died, and he finally wore the crown. Nicknamed *Philometor* (Mama's boy), his interests lay in gardening and studying botany and medicine. He was engaged to a woman named Berenice, a princess of Egypt, but she died, with rumors he murdered her.

After ruling five years, Attalus III died in 133 BCE with no children. He predicted Rome would take Pergamon at his death, so, to prevent bloodshed, he bequeathed Pergamon to Rome before he died. Before Rome took possession, Aristonicus, claiming to be Eumenes II's illegitimate son, snatched the throne.

Aristonicus enjoyed initial success in his insurgency, even killing the Roman consul Crassus and vanquishing his army. But the Roman consul Perperna dealt a blow to the rebel forces in 129 BCE, starving them into surrender. Aristonicus was paraded through the streets of Rome and then strangled. The Roman consul Aquillius divided the Pergamon kingdom between Rome, Cappadocia, and Pontus.

The last Diadochi – Seleucus I Nicator – founded the Seleucid Empire from his share of Alexander the Great's empire. Seleucus received the Mesopotamian area of Babylon, which he brilliantly and ruthlessly expanded to include a mammoth section of Alexander's former Near Eastern territories. The Seleucid Empire encompassed present-day Afghanistan, Iran, Iraq, Israel, Jordan, Kuwait, Lebanon, Syria, Turkmenistan, and Turkey at its apex.

The Seleucid Empire evolved into a dominant Hellenistic center. The empire tolerated local customs, but a Greek elite controlled the politics, and the people spoke Koine Greek, along with Aramaic or other regional languages. Massive immigration into the Seleucid Empire from Greece impacted the empire's ethnicity and culture. The Seleucid's major Hellenistic rival – Ptolemaic Egypt – often contested the western Seleucid provinces.

From 305-303 BCE, Seleucus clashed with the Maurya Empire of the Indian subcontinent, whose emperor Chandragupta conquered Alexander's former Greek satraps in the Indus. Seleucus crossed the Indus River to meet Chandragupta's army and 9000 war elephants. After initially engaging in battle on the Indus' banks, they decided an alliance was a better idea. Seleucus gave his daughter in marriage to Chandragupta in exchange for 500 war elephants. Those were the elephants Seleucus used to defeat Antigonus I in the epic Battle of Ipsus – in which Seleucus gained eastern Turkey and northern Syria.

On Syria's Orontes River, Seleucus founded his capital city of Antioch, which became the center of Hellenistic Judaism and later the "cradle of Christianity." His plans to conquer Thrace and Macedonia were interrupted when Ptolemy Ceraunus murdered him. Seleucus' son Antiochus I Soter inherited a colossal empire, but holding it together proved a challenge for him and his son Antiochus II Theos – with repeated invasions by Ptolemy II of Egypt and a flood of Celts into the northern borders.

While Antiochus II was battling Egypt, several of his provinces proclaimed independence: Bactria, Sogdiana, Cappadocia, and Parthia. Antiochus finally made peace with Ptolemy II of Egypt – who gave him his daughter Berenice in marriage. This political marriage forced Antiochus to divorce his first wife Laodice, bypassing their children in favor of Berenice's children inheriting the crown. Within a few years, Laodice successfully lured Antiochus away from Berenice and their baby Antiochus – and then poisoned him! Her co-conspirators murdered Berenice and her son, and Laodice's son Seleucus II became king.

Ptolemy III crushed Seleucus II in the Third Syrian War, and the empire's borders continued to crumble – giving way to the Celtic Galatians and Pergamon. Seleucus' son Antiochus III (the Great) was the one that plotted with Philip V of Macedon to grab Egypt's territories from the 6-year-old Pharoah – which proved successful for Antiochus in regaining Syria and Israel. When Rome defeated Philip, Antiochus took advantage of the power vacuum and invaded Thrace – allying with the Aetolian League. However, the Romans showed up, swiftly trouncing him and ending any aspirations for taking Greece.

Antiochus IV called himself Epiphanes (God manifest); his detractors called him Epimames (insane).

https://commons.wikimedia.org/wiki/File:Antiochus_IV_Epiphanes.jpg

Antiochus III's son – Antiochus IV Epiphanes – was waging a successful battle against Egypt when the Roman Proconsul Popilius arrived with tablets holding the Roman Senate's decree: "Withdraw from Egypt or consider yourself at war with Rome."

Antiochus IV said he would call a council, but Popilius took a stick and drew a circle around Antiochus in the sand. "Don't step out of that circle until you give me a reply to take back to the Senate!"

Antiochus withdrew, humiliated. Simmering with rage, he passed through Judea, attacking Jerusalem, killing Ptolemy's supporters, and viciously ravaging the city. He slaughtered men, women, children, and babies – 40,000 in three days, taking another 40,000 as captive slaves. He outlawed the Jewish faith and ordered the priests to worship Zeus in the Jewish Temple – which they refused to do. He defiled the temple by sacrificing a pig – an unclean animal for the Jews. This "abomination of desolation" (Daniel 12:11) triggered the Maccabean Revolt in which the Jews recaptured Jerusalem, declared Judea independent and cleansed the temple. To this day, Jews celebrate Hanukkah (Chanukah) in remembrance.

Following Antiochus' death, the Seleucid Empire continued to decay with internecine conflicts. Under Mithridates I's spectacular leadership, the nomadic Iranian Parthians conquered lands extending from the Euphrates to the Indus River. Tigranes the Great of Armenia invaded Syria, crowning himself king in 83 BCE. In 69 BCE, the Roman general Lucullus defeated the Tigranes and Mithridates. Still, multiple civil wars continued to rock the former Seleucid Empire, weakening it until most western provinces fell under Roman control.

In 63 BCE, the great Roman general Pompey – who later became part of Rome's Triumvirate with Julius Caesar and Crassus – reorganized and consolidated the one-time Seleucid empire into Roman provinces. Some provinces continued as semi-independent client-states, such as Armenia, where King Tigranes remained on his throne. Pompey conquered Syria's cities, with Damascus' fall completing his campaign in Syria – transforming it into a Roman province.

Finally, he came to Judea, currently in a bitter conflict between two royal brothers. Goaded by the wily Antipater the Idumean, Hyrcanus II called on King Aretas of Arabia to help him get his throne back from his brother Aristobulus II. Arriving to find the Arabians besieging Jerusalem, Pompey promptly dispatched Aretes and placed Judea under Roman control. Julius Caesar arrived in 47 BCE, assigning Antipater as Roman Procurator. Antipater's son Herod was infamous for the massacre of the infants in Bethlehem after Jesus' birth.

For three centuries, Egypt's pharaohs were Macedonians – descendants of Ptolemy – the general of Alexander the Great. Alexandria became Egypt's new capital and the premier center of Hellenistic culture. The Ptolemies expanded Egypt's territories into Libya, Nubia, and the Sinai. Ptolemy I and his descendants adopted Egyptian dress to gain legitimacy, the pharaohs married their sisters per Egyptian custom, and the Greeks incorporated Egyptian religion into their belief system. Egypt was the most powerful and affluent Hellenistic kingdom until it weakened from sordid quarrels and intrigue among the royal family. As Egypt diminished in power, Rome grew in strength, giving Egypt no choice but to ally with Rome.

In Rome, Pompey had fallen out with Julius Caesar, and Crassus died fighting the Parthians - dissolving the Triumvirate - and placing Pompey and Caesar in a power struggle for Rome's leadership. Pompey left Rome for Greece, drumming up support from Greek leaders he'd helped in the Mithridatic War for his campaign against Julius Caesar, setting up his base in Macedonia.

Julius Caesar caught up with him on Thessaly's plains, outmaneuvering and defeating Pompey's forces. Pompey raced to the coast and sailed to Egypt, while Caesar pardoned all Pompey's men who surrendered. Pompey expected refuge in Egypt, but the Egyptians had two Roman mercenaries kill him, presenting his head to Caesar when he arrived a few days later. Even though Pompey was his rival, Caesar considered the murder of a Roman general and ruler an affront - especially from an ally. He also took it personally - Pompey had once been his son-in-law and co-ruler. The Egyptians must pay!

According to tradition, Cleopatra was smuggled into Julius Caesar's quarters wrapped in a rug.

https://en.wikipedia.org/wiki/Cleopatra#/media/File:Cleopatra_and_Caesar_by_Jean-Leon-Gerome.jpg

And then Caesar met the enchanting Cleopatra. Forgetting Pompey, forgetting Rome, he fell under her spell and got entangled in the imbroglio involving Cleopatra VII and her husband (and brother) – the 13-year-old Pharoah Ptolemy XIII. Caesar forced Ptolemy to reinstate his sister-wife to Egypt's throne. Ptolemy XIII then allied with another sister Arsinoe and civil war broke out in Alexandria. The Library of Alexandria caught fire – precious documents from antiquity were destroyed. Caesar and Cleopatra won the ensuing Battle of the Nile in 47 BCE, and Ptolemy XIII fled Alexandria, drowning in the Nile.

Cleopatra married another younger brother, the 12-year-old Ptolemy XIV, and also, in 47 BCE, gave birth to Julius Caesar's only biological son: Caesarion. Cleopatra was living with Caesar in Rome when several senators assassinated him in 44 BCE. Cleopatra quickly fled back to Egypt, and her younger brother/second husband, Ptolemy XIV, died of mysterious circumstances four months later. Caesarion, Cleopatra's three-year-old son by Caesar, became co-Pharoah with her.

Caesar's adopted son Octavian marched on Rome in 43 BCE, proclaiming himself consul and forming the Second Triumvirate with Mark Antony and Lepidus. Antony got the eastern provinces and used Ephesus as his base. In 41 BCE, Antony invited Cleopatra to meet him in Tarsus to sort out Egypt's alliance with Rome. Cleopatra made a sensational entrance, arrayed as the Greek goddess of love Aphrodite and sailing up the river in a magical boat with a golden prow, purple sails, and silver oars. Captivated, Anthony fell passionately in love, and Cleopatra gave birth to their twins the next year: Cleopatra Selene and Alexander Helios.

Meanwhile, Antony's jealous wife Fulvia was stirring up an insurgency in Rome – which failed; exiled to Greece, she met with a highly irritated Antony and died of mysterious circumstances shortly after. Anthony returned to Rome to smooth things over with his co-ruler Octavian, marrying Octavian's sister Octavia just weeks after Fulvia's death. Antony headed to Parthia on a campaign with his new wife, but Octavian only sent half the troops he'd promised, and the campaign turned into a calamity. Octavian needed more men! Where could he get them?

Cleopatra had a large army at her disposal, so Antony sent Octavia back to Rome and picked up his steamy affair with Cleopatra. He awarded Armenia to their son Alexander Helios and named Cleopatra Queen of Kings. Cleopatra gave birth to another son – Ptolemy Philadelphus – in 36 BCE.

Back in Rome, Antony's co-ruler Octavian, furious that Antony had abandoned his daughter for Cleopatra, stormed the Vestal Virgins' temple where he'd heard Antony had hidden his will. He discovered Antony's plan to bequeath even more Roman provinces to his sons. Worse yet, Antony named Cleopatra's son Caesarion as Caesar's legitimate son and heir, which would place Caesarion over Octavian as ruler of Rome. When Octavian published the will's contents, the Senate voted in 32 BCE to go to war against Cleopatra – but one-third of the Senate and both consuls supported Antony and sailed over to his side of the sea.

Cleopatra and Antony pitted their navy against Octavian's in the 31 BCE Battle of Actium. Outmaneuvered by Rome's Commander Agrippa, the lovers fled back to Egypt. When Octavian besieged Egypt the following year, Antony plunged his sword into his chest, dying in Cleopatra's arms. Unable to bear the thought of being paraded through Rome's streets in chains, Cleopatra clasped a viper to her breast and died from its bite. Octavian buried her next to Antony, but he killed her son Caesarion by Caesar – the last of the Ptolemaic rulers. He paraded Cleopatra's other children by Antony through Rome in golden chains, then gave them to his sister Octavia – Antony's wife – to rear.

Roman Egypt was among Rome's wealthiest provinces, and Alexandria remained the hub of Hellenistic culture and a leading city of the Mediterranean into the Middle Ages. Rome's main interest in Egypt was as a reliable source of grain. Rome did not change the Egyptian governmental system except by replacing Greeks with Romans in more prestigious offices. Greeks continued with middle-management in Egypt's government, and Koine Greek remained the governmental language until the Muslims invaded in the seventh century.

Conclusion

"We are all Greeks. Our laws, our literature, our religion, our arts have their root in Greece."

~ Percy Bysshe Shelley, *Hellas*

Our world continues to reap the benefits of the invaluable and ingenious contributions of the Greeks to astronomy, mathematics, medicine, and philosophy. Greek philosophy and literature still influence our worldview and core values. Greek aesthetics live on in modern architecture, sculpture, and art. Greek culture dramatically shaped the Roman Empire, Egypt, the Middle East, and Asia – and it has passed its legacy to us today.

Our thoughts inevitably drift to erudite, aesthetic Athens and disciplined, intransigent Sparta when we think of ancient Greece. Once Greece's two most powerful city-states, usually rivals but occasionally allies, their disparate worldviews and social-political structures led them down different paths. The Athenians were innovative, adaptable, and progressive – and their city survived into the modern world – and thrived! The Spartans were courageous but conservative to a fault – unwilling to change their ways in a changing world.

As modern Greece's capital and largest city, Athens is a dynamic center of culture, economics, finance, and politics – much as it was in ancient times. It still symbolizes art, democracy, and freedom. King Otto of Greece rebuilt modern-day Sparta (Sparti) in 1834 with a neo-classical architectural model, and once again, it is the administrative, cultural, and economic center of Laconia. And it's still the most conservative city in Greece!

Surrounded by water, the maritime Greeks traded and set up independent city-states around the Mediterranean, stretching from France and Spain to North Africa and the Middle East – then progressing through the Dardanelles and Bosporus Straits into the Black Sea. The Greeks imported their culture throughout this massive global segment and assimilated artistic styles and techniques from other lands. Through Alexander the Great's exploits, Greek influence pressed further – into the Indus Valley and southeast Asia.

The exchange of ideas between Greek, North African, and Near Eastern scholars created an explosion of mathematical understanding, scientific exploration, and medical progress. Literature, art, theater, architecture, and philosophy reached new heights. The Greeks encountered new beliefs: Buddhism, Hinduism, Zoroastrianism, Judaism, and Egyptian religion. Hellenistic Jews like Philo embraced and developed Greek thought, pointing out that Greek philosophical concepts – such as the *logos*, Zeno's idea of the wise man, and Plato's theory of form – had already been laid out in the Tanakh (Old Testament).

The Greeks were polytheistic – worshipping gods with human characteristics who could and did marry, cheat on their spouses, bear children, and regularly deceive and fight with each other. Their antics impelled some Greek philosophers – including Xenophanes, Socrates, Anaxagoras, Plato, and Aristotle – to lean toward some form of monotheism with a divinely perfect God, arguing that if the gods weren't virtuous, what hope had humanity?

This theological shift influenced the receptivity of the Greeks to Persian Zoroastrianism and Hellenistic Judaism. Alexander even assigned a Jewish quarter – literally one-fourth of the city – when he founded Alexandria, Egypt. Later, Christianity was exceptionally well-received in the Greek world, rapidly spreading through the Greek cities around the Mediterranean: Antioch and Damascus in Syria, Berea and Thessalonica in Macedonia, Syracuse in Sicily, Miletus and Galatia in Asia Minor, the islands of Crete and Cyprus, and many more.

Before Rome conquered the Greek cities and kingdoms, its art and culture were already immensely influential to Rome. As Rome interacted more with Greeks during campaigns in the east and then ruled over them, they soaked up Greek politics, religion, philosophy, science, and the arts all the more. In the words of Horace, "Captive Greece took captive her fierce conqueror and instilled her arts in rustic Latium."

As Rome freely borrowed from Greek civilization, the joint culture became known as Greco-Roman culture or Classical civilization – which formed the core of architecture, art, engineering, language, law, and literature for western civilization. Roman artists, poets, architects, and philosophers adapted Hellenistic models, creating their own style conveying solidity and strength.

The Lincoln Memorial in Washington D.C. was modeled after Athens' Parthenon.

https://commons.wikimedia.org/wiki/File:LincolnMemorial_DC.jpg

Greek culture left its legacy on the Roman Empire, the Byzantine Empire, the Christian church, the Renaissance of western Europe, and the Neoclassicist movement in Europe and America. The Greeks pioneered a democratic government that directly influenced the formation of the United States of America's new government. Many key buildings in Washington D.C. reflect Classical Greek architecture, including the Capitol building, the Supreme Court, and the Lincoln Memorial.

Greek art and sculpture influenced Renaissance art, such as Raphael's *School of Athens* fresco in the Vatican, Michelangelo's *Creation of Adam* fresco on the Sistine Chapel's ceiling, or his *David* sculpture. Byzantine architecture followed Greco-Roman influences and impacted medieval European architecture, specifically Renaissance and Ottoman traditions.

Hellenistic philosophy influenced Christian theology – and vice-versa. The Apostle Paul's debate with the Epicurean and Stoic philosophers at Athens' Areopagus demonstrated his Hellenistic education as he quoted Greek philosophers and poets (Acts 17:16-34). In *The Confessions,* Saint Augustine of Hippo talked about Plato's shadows in the cave, saying God is the light that created the shadows; to know God is to understand reality, while those who deny God remain in the cave, seeing only the dim shadows of the real world.

The Greek language has the longest documented history of any Indo-European language – 34 centuries! The Mycenaean-era written language in a syllabic script was lost in Greece's Dark Ages. Greeks adopted an alphabet in the Archaic period, and several regional dialects were spoken in the Archaic and Classical periods. By the Hellenistic period, the common Koine Greek was read and spoken throughout the Greek world.

Greek continued as the lingua franca in the eastern Roman empire throughout the Roman age, although Latin was also used – especially for government functions. Judaism and Christianity helped keep the Greek language alive through the Septuagint translation of the Old Testament and the New Testament written in Koine Greek. Worship in eastern Christian churches used a Greek liturgy, and writings of many early church fathers (up to around 400 CE) were in Greek. These included Justin Martyr (who was Greek), Papias of Hierapolis (also Greek), and the Cappadocian Fathers.

The Byzantine Empire was the eastern part of the Roman Empire – the part that survived when the western part of the Roman Empire fell – including Rome. The Byzantine Empire ruled for another 1000 years until it fell to the Ottoman Empire in 1453 CE. Even during the Roman Empire, the eastern section continued speaking and writing Greek, except for government and military affairs in Latin.

After the western Roman Empire collapsed, the remaining Byzantine Empire gradually used more Greek for governmental functions. Greek became the sole official language in the seventh century CE and continued until the fall of the Byzantine empire in the 15th century. This "Byzantine Greek" or "Medieval Greek" gradually evolved into the modern Greek used today.

What have we as a modern society learned and acquired from the Ancient Greeks? We owe our understanding of science and mathematics to the Classical and Hellenistic Greeks, whose philosophy emphasized logic and championed rational, impartial observation of the world around us. The Greeks gave us most of our foundational concepts of geometry, our first astronomical models, and the beginnings of modern medicine using an empirical, systematic diagnosis of diseases.

In sculptures, paintings, and mosaics, Greeks captured the human form realistically and movingly - like nothing ever seen before - but today easily recognizable. The distinctive Greek architecture - especially stunning pillars - persists today around the world. Our concepts of democracy and trial by jury are a Greek legacy. Let's not forget the Olympic Games! The Greeks began the tradition of setting aside ethnic and political differences to gather peacefully for the pure joy of competing in sports - something we still enjoy today. And what would modern civilization be like without Greek food?

Why is knowing Greek history so important? It unlocks the door to an ancient past that has reached through time to touch all parts of our lives. Through knowing Greek history, we understand why we think the way we do, why we perceive God and the universe the way we do, why we do politics the way we do, and why we perceive artistic beauty the way we do. Knowledge of Greece's past deepens our understanding of the literature, art, political systems, and philosophies that surround us today.

"What you leave behind is not what is engraved in stone monuments,

but what is woven into the lives of others."

~ Pericles

Here's another book by Enthralling History that you might like

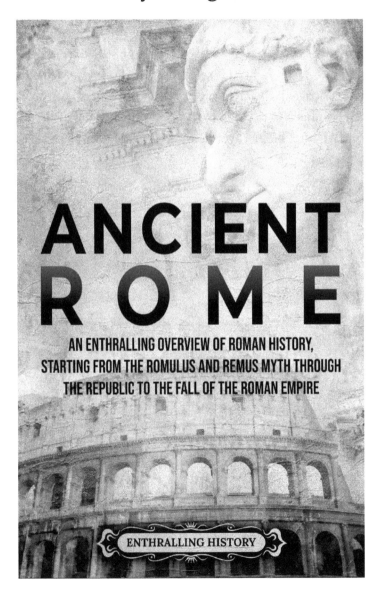

Free limited time bonus

Stop for a moment. We have a free bonus set up for you. The problem is this: we forget 90% of everything that we read after 7 days. Crazy fact, right? Here's the solution: we've created a printable, 1-page pdf summary for this book that you're reading now. All you have to do to get your free pdf summary is to go to the following website: **https://livetolearn.lpages.co/enthrallinghistory/**

Once you do, it will be intuitive. Enjoy, and thank you!

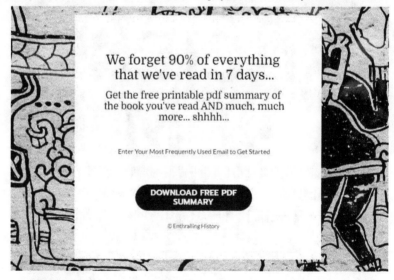

We forget 90% of everything that we've read in 7 days...

Get the free printable pdf summary of the book you've read AND much, much more... shhhh...

Enter Your Most Frequently Used Email to Get Started

DOWNLOAD FREE PDF SUMMARY

© Enthralling History

Bibliography

Arrian. *Alexander the Great: The Anabasis and the Indica.* Translated by Martin Hammond. Oxford: Oxford University Press, 2013.

Austin, M. M. "Greek Tyrants and the Persians, 546-479 B. C." *The Classical Quarterly* 40, no. 2 (1990): 289-306. Accessed September 6, 2021. http://www.jstor.org/stable/639090.

Barron, John P. "The Sixth-Century Tyranny at Samos." *The Classical Quarterly* 14, no. 2 (1964): 210-29. Accessed September 1, 2021. http://www.jstor.org/stable/637725.

Bennett, Bob and Mike Roberts. *The Wars of Alexander's Successors, 323–281 BC (Commanders and Campaigns Book 1).* South Yorkshire: Pen & Sword Military, 2013.

Bennett, Bob and Mike Roberts. *The Wars of Alexander's Successors 323 – 281 BC. Volume 2: Battles and Tactics.* South Yorkshire: Pen & Sword Military, 2009.

Cartledge, Paul. *The Spartans: The World of the Warrior-Heroes of Ancient Greece.* New York: The Overlook Press, 2003.

Dillon, John and Lloyd P. Gerson. *Neoplatonic Philosophy: Introductory Readings.* Cambridge, MA: Hackett Publishing Company, 2004.

Figueira, Thomas J. "Population Patterns in Late Archaic and Classical Sparta." *Transactions of the American Philological Association* 116 (1986): 165–213. https://doi.org/10.2307/283916.

Guthrie, W. K. C. *A History of Greek Philosophy; Revised Edition books I & II.* Cambridge: Cambridge University Press, 1979.

Guthrie, W. K. C. *The Sophists; Reprint Edition.* Cambridge: Cambridge University Press; 1977.

Hack, Harold M. "Thebes and the Spartan Hegemony, 386-382 B.C." *The American Journal of Philology* 99, no. 2 (1978): 210–27. https://doi.org/10.2307/293647.

Heidel, William Arthur. "Anaximander's Book, the Earliest Known Geographical Treatise." *Proceedings of the American Academy of Arts and Sciences* 56, no. 7 (1921): 239-88. Accessed September 5, 2021. doi:10.2307/20025852.

Henderson, W.J. "The Nature and Function of Solon's Poetry: Fr. Diehl, 4 West." *Acta Classica 25* (1982): 21-33. Accessed September 2, 2021. http://www.jstor.org/stable/24591787.

Herodotus, *The Histories.* Translated by Tom Holland. New York: Penguin Classics, 2015.

Homer. *The Iliad.* Translated by Samuel Butler. Internet Classics Archive. http://classics.mit.edu/Homer/iliad.html

Homer. *The Odyssey.* Translated by Samuel Butler. Internet Classics Archive. http://classics.mit.edu/Homer/odyssey.html

Isocrates. *Letters.* Perseus Digital Library. Tufts University. http://www.perseus.tufts.edu/hopper/text?doc=Perseus:text:1999.01.0246:letter=3.

Long, A. A. *Hellenistic Philosophy: Stoics, Epicureans, Sceptics.* California: University of California Press, 1986.

Matyszak, Philip. *Greece Against Rome: The Fall of the Hellenistic Kingdoms 250–31 BC.* South Yorkshire: Pen & Sword Military, 2020.